The Celtic World

Jennifer Paxton, Ph.D.

PUBLISHED BY:

THE GREAT COURSES
Corporate Headquarters
4840 Westfields Boulevard, Suite 500
Chantilly, Virginia 20151-2299
Phone: 1-800-832-2412
Fax: 703-378-3819
www.thegreatcourses.com

Copyright © The Teaching Company, 2018

Printed in the United States of America

This book is in copyright. All rights reserved.

Without limiting the rights under copyright reserved above,
no part of this publication may be reproduced, stored in
or introduced into a retrieval system, or transmitted,
in any form, or by any means
(electronic, mechanical, photocopying, recording, or otherwise),
without the prior written permission of
The Teaching Company.

Jennifer Paxton, Ph.D.

Director of the University Honors Program and Clinical Assistant Professor of History
The Catholic University of America

Jennifer Paxton is the director of the University Honors Program and a Clinical Assistant Professor of History at The Catholic University of America. She was previously a Professorial Lecturer in History at Georgetown University, where she taught for more than a decade. Dr. Paxton received her doctorate in History from Harvard University, where she has also taught and earned a Certificate of Distinction in Teaching. She is a widely published, award-winning writer and a highly regarded scholar, earning both a Mellon Fellowship in the Humanities and a Frank Knox Memorial Traveling Fellowship.

Dr. Paxton lectures regularly at the Smithsonian Institution and serves as a study leader to Scotland and Ireland for Smithsonian Journeys. Her research focuses on England from the reign of King Alfred to the late 12th century, particularly the intersection between the authority of church and state and the representation of the past in historical texts, especially those produced by religious communities. She is completing a book that examines how monastic historians shaped their narratives to project present polemical concerns onto the past.

Dr. Paxton's other Great Courses are *The Story of Medieval England: From King Arthur to the Tudor Conquest* and *1066: The Year That Changed Everything*. ■

Table of Contents

Introduction
Professor Biography i
Course Scope 1

Lecture Guides

Lecture 1
Who Are the Celts? 4

Lecture 2
The Celts and the Classical World. 14

Lecture 3
Celtic Art and Artifacts 24

Lecture 4
Celtic Languages in the Ancient World 33

Lecture 5
Caesar and the Gauls 42

Lecture 6
Celtic Religion and the Druids 54

Lecture 7
Celtic Britain and Roman Britain 64

Lecture 8
    Celts and the Picts in Scotland 75

Lecture 9
    Prehistoric Ireland and the Celts 85

Lecture 10
    Celtic Britain after Rome 94

Lecture 11
    Brittany and Galicia: Fringe of the Fringe 101

Lecture 12
    Celtic Churches 113

Lecture 13
    Celtic Art and Insular Art 124

Lecture 14
    Medieval Irish Literature 134

Lecture 15
    Celtic Women, Families, and Social Structure. 143

Lecture 16
    The Irish Sea World: Celts and Vikings 152

Lecture 17
    English Invasions of Wales and Ireland. 161

Lecture 18
    Scotland from *Macbeth* to *Braveheart*. 172

Lecture 19
   Politics and Literature in Wales 184

Lecture 20
   The Tudor Conquest of Ireland 193

Lecture 21
   (Re)Discovering the Celts 204

Lecture 22
   The Gaelic Revival in Ireland............................. 213

Lecture 23
   Celtic Music and Dance................................. 222

Lecture 24
   The Celts Today....................................... 232

Supplemental Material
   Bibliography... 243

   Image Credits 255

The Celtic World

The term *Celtic* often evokes two different and not entirely compatible images. One is that of the ancient warriors who rampaged across Europe and terrified the Greeks and Romans; the other is of the warm, welcoming nations on the fringes of Europe known for their music, arts, poetry, and spirituality. Are these really the same people, and if so, how did one evolve into the other?

The answer, as it turns out, is complicated. The story we had for a long time was of a single, unified cultural group that emerged in the central part of Europe, migrated westward, and were finally all but pushed off the continent by conflict with Roman legions and Germanic tribes. However, over the past several decades, new research in archaeology, linguistics, and even DNA has revealed surprising new information—and raised quite a few more questions—about who the Celts really were and are.

In these 24 lectures, we will examine what we now know about the Celtic world. The course is roughly divided into three parts—ancient, medieval, and modern—and will examine a variety of evidence through multiple perspectives.

We will begin by debunking some of the most common myths about the ancient Celts. Then, we will examine the textual evidence about the Celts that comes to us from classical writers, including Julius Caesar. We will next consider how the texts line up with the archaeological and linguistic evidence and consider whether we can form a reliable model of what it meant to be a Celt.

From there, we will look at the geography of the Celtic world and how Celtic characteristics manifested differently in different regions. We will look first at the Gauls of what is now France; then at the Britons, Picts, Irish, Scots, and other groups in the British Isles; and finally at the Bretons and Galicians on the remote western edges of Europe. We will consider their origins, their relationships, and their unique contributions to the Celtic phenomenon. Along the way, we will visit with the druids—perhaps the most myth-shrouded and misunderstood people in all of Celtic culture.

From these ancient origins, we will turn to the medieval Celts, beginning with the most influential of all medieval institutions: the church. We will look at the similarities and differences in beliefs and practices between the Celtic and Roman churches, and study how they diverged and reunited. Then, we will look at the art and literature of medieval Celtic society, its popularity both within and beyond the Celtic realms, and its influence on the rest of Europe. We will also consider the social and political institutions of the Celtic world and see how kinship ties pervaded every aspect of society.

Next, we will study how the Celts interacted with their neighbors—namely, the Vikings and the English—and see how the contacts and clashes among these groups challenged traditional Celtic ways of life. We will consider how these conflicts set the stage for many of the aspects of modern Celtic society. We will examine the intersection of art and politics in some of the most interesting and influential literature of medieval Europe—that of the Welsh. Finally, we will see how the Tudor monarchs firmly—if not permanently—brought Ireland under English control, setting the stage for the modern era.

The idea of Celtic identity as we know it today was largely developed by historians, writers, and artists of the Celtic Revival movement, which began in the late 16th century and arguably continues to this day. We will look at some of the most influential thinkers in the Celtic Revival movement and some of the most important phenomena—some of which may be surprising.

No course on the Celtic world would be complete without a look at one of most widespread and beloved aspects of Celtic culture: its music. We will consider the traditional forms and the modern manifestations, as well as the related art of Celtic dance.

Finally, we will look at the Celtic world today: How do the Celts define their identity, what do they value, and where are they headed? We will look back on what we learned throughout the course and ask who the "real" Celts are, or whether that question even matters. We may not be able to answer all of these questions, but even the remaining mysteries will leave us with a greater appreciation for the world of the Celts—their history, their culture, and their ongoing influence. ■

Lecture 1

Who Are the Celts?

This course has two stories to tell: one that takes place in the heart of Europe and one that takes place on the periphery of Europe. The course explores the connection between these two phenomena: the fierce warriors of the continent who gave the Romans a challenge and the residents of Ireland and the other Celtic realms who kept ancient traditions alive in the face of relentless pressure from centralizing monarchies, especially England and France. This course will also tell the story of how those traditions were spread around the world by emigrants from the Celtic realms.

Celtic Culture

- Some of these phenomena are readily recognizable as Celtic in origin: the shamrock, the Celtic cross, the mischievous leprechaun and his pot of gold at the end of the rainbow, the banshee who wails mysteriously to signal a death, the Highland bagpipe, and the tartan, among many others.

- But some elements of Celtic tradition and vocabulary have been incorporated into modern western culture so thoroughly that the Celtic origins of certain words and customs are not readily known. For instance, many words have come into English from the Irish language, which is sometimes referred to outside of Ireland as Gaelic. For example, the words *phony* and *smithereens* have Irish origins.

- For many people, Celtic culture really means Irish culture. Irish culture has of course been spread around the globe by the Irish diaspora, the many millions of people who trace their descent to the island of Ireland. Lots of people who find themselves fascinated by Irish culture do not have Irish heritage; they just like Irish music and dancing. Think of the enormous success of the Irish dancing show *Riverdance* or the popularity of singers such as Enya.

- Irish writers have also made a huge impact on the world. Four Irish authors have won Nobel Prizes for literature, a remarkable achievement considering that the entire population of Ireland, north and south, is only seven million. That's less than one percent of the population of Europe.

- Celtic art styles have also become popular around the world. The dense abstract patterns familiar from the medieval Irish manuscript the *Book of Kells* can now be found on everything from tea towels to t-shirts to tattoos.

- The reach of Irish culture of course extends beyond the realm of the fine arts. There are Irish pubs in every corner of the globe, from Hong Kong to Buenos Aires, and St. Patrick's Day parades can be found almost

everywhere. Millions and millions of people take pleasure in wearing green and declaring themselves Irish for a day.

- But there is a major paradox at the heart of the Celtic craze. The Celtic realms themselves are tiny. The island of Ireland itself has a population of only about six and a half million people, but it contains two political entities: the Republic of Ireland and Northern Ireland, which is a part of the United Kingdom.

- In total, the areas that identify themselves now as part of the Celtic world—what some people call the Celtic Fringe—have a combined population of only around 20 million people. So how did the Celtic phenomenon spread so far and wide? That is one of the main questions this course will try to answer.

A Version of Celtic History

- According to the version of Celtic history this course's professor originally learned, the Celts are a people who arose in central Europe in the middle of the first millennium BC. There, they created a culture that produced a particular art style that focused on beautiful abstract patterns and stylized animals.

- But besides being artists, they were also dedicated warriors, determined to win glory in battle. The Celts spread out from their Central European homelands throughout Europe. When they campaigned to the south and the east, they clashed with the Romans and the Greeks, who wrote the first descriptions we have of them, some of which are truly bloodcurdling.

- In addition to sacking the city of Rome in 390 BC, the Celts desecrated the shrine of Delphi in Greece, the home of the famous oracle, in 279 BC. Afterward, they established themselves in central Anatolia, which is now Turkey, becoming the ancestors of the Galatians that we know of from the New Testament.

- The Celts also spread west, into Gaul (what is now France) and down into Spain. Then, around 200 BC or so, they took to the seas and invaded Britain and Ireland, where they conquered the native inhabitants and established their own culture and language.

- At one point, then, the Celts dominated most of the continent of Europe, even extending down into northern Italy, where the Romans were hard pressed to restrain their advances. A map of Europe would show a uniform Celtic hegemony from Ireland to Greece and from Spain to Austria.

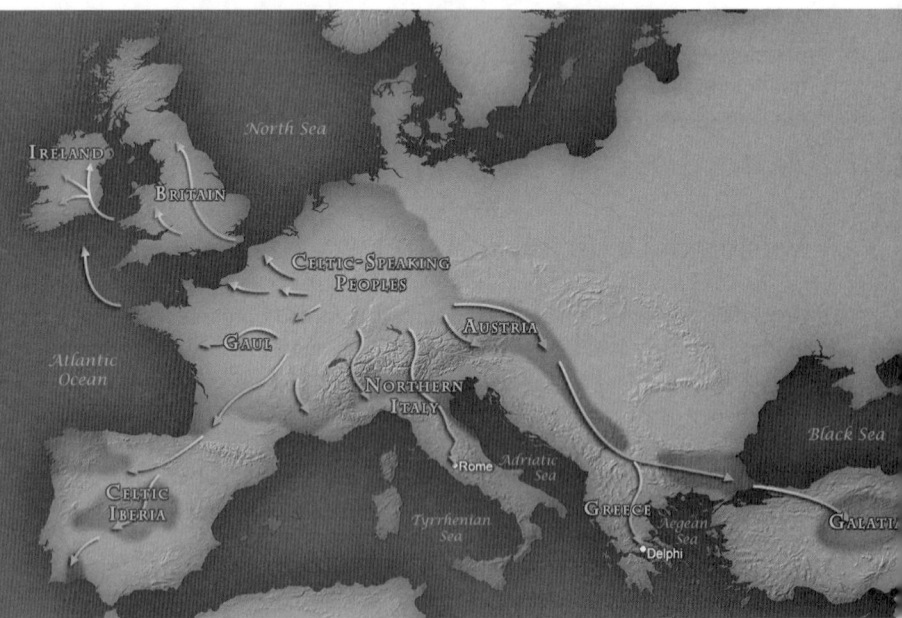

- But then, the tide turned against the Celts. Slowly, the Romans pushed the Celts back. The Romans conquered Spain first, then Gaul, and finally Britain, though they never managed to subdue the entire island. They left the wild north of Britain, what is now Scotland, unconquered, and they never even tried to conquer Ireland. But when the Romans were forced to withdraw from Britain, the Celts took up arms again and bravely fought a series of unsuccessful battles against a new group of invaders, the Anglo-Saxons.

- The Celts were driven into the more remote corners of the island of Britain: the beautiful, mountainous north and west and southwest. Some of them migrated to western France to the region now known as Brittany, and even to northern Spain, where some remnants of Celtic populations also survived. These regions on the periphery of Western Europe, along with the entire island of Ireland, became known much later as the Celtic Fringe.

- Thus, the story goes, only in these remote parts of Britain and in Ireland, plus Brittany and northern Spain, did the original Celtic civilization that had once covered most of Europe manage to survive. Over the centuries, the Celts clung to their cultural autonomy by cultivating their distinctive traditions in music and literature and art. All the while, they progressively came to be dominated by the strong nation-states that arose in England, France, and Spain.

- This version of the history of the Celts as a people that once ruled Europe has been enormously influential in the modern world. However, recent scholarship has uncovered evidence that the story is much more complicated, and more interesting, than we used to think.

A More Complicated Version

- It is becoming clearer and clearer that the definition of *Celtic* is much harder to pin down than scholars have traditionally believed. Several key traits—primarily their language, their art, and their social and military customs—have usually identified the Celts, as we read about them in the works written about the Celts by Greek and Roman authors.

- The idea has been that the Celts came with a Celtic cultural package: all Celts spoke Celtic languages, produced Celtic art, and did stereotypically Celtic things, like, for instance, collecting and revering severed human heads.

- Today, we associate the Celts primarily with Ireland and the British Isles. The trouble is that modern scholarship is causing the Celtic hypothesis to unravel. It turns out that the peoples of Ireland and Britain may have had no ethnic connection to the peoples on the continent of Europe. Scholars no longer believe that there was one unified Celtic culture spread by a specific group of people who shared a common genetic descent.

- Instead, it looks as though the traits we associate with the Celts today, such as their language and their art, may have spread around Europe to various peoples who had no genetic connection to each other, and these characteristics may not have started in the same place.

- The art we think of as Celtic may have developed in one part of Europe, while the language we think of as Celtic may have developed in another part of Europe. It is no longer necessarily the case that we can pin one specific set of cultural features to one specific group of people. This new scholarly approach to the Celts flies in the face of centuries of settled beliefs about where the Celts came from and how they spread.

- Note that something is definitely lost if we abandon the old model. The earlier idea has Celts on the move, conquering Europe and then surviving against all odds in Ireland and the fringes of Britain. This makes the Celts look extremely powerful, and it gives them a kind of romantic status as the last remnants of a lost civilization. But the problem with the model is that it's probably not true.

- There is very little evidence to support the idea that there ever was a strictly Celtic civilization. People from different parts of the so-called Celtic world in 200 BC probably wouldn't have understood the question if they were asked if they were Celts. People in Ireland would have had no notion of being part of a unified civilization that extended all the way to the Galatians in Turkey.

- At the start of a course about the Celts, it may seem surprising to attack the very idea of identifying the Celts as one unified people. But rest assured: the Celtic phenomenon is even more interesting than the old model would suggest.

- We are left with three fascinating questions this course will examine:

  1. What happened among the disparate peoples who have been identified as Celtic to make them adopt the cultural traits that we associate now with Celticness? In other words, how do cultural identities form in the first place?

  2. If the Celts were not a united people, how did this idea of the Celts as a single people arise in the first place?

  3. Why has the culture that came to be associated with the Celts been so successful around the world?

Evidence

- To tell the story of the Celts, this course will discuss several kinds of evidence. Scholars like to talk in terms of evidence, which is simply the material they use to create a picture of what happened in the past.

- History is this course's professor's own discipline. The most important method used by historians is the analysis of written texts. We can learn a lot about the Celts from the works written by the ancient Romans and Greeks who encountered them. The ways in which we analyze texts can change over time. History is a discipline that is always renewing itself.

- Textual analysis has many drawbacks as well as advantages. We are limited by what remains. There are many things we'd like to know about the past, but if nobody chose to write them down, or if texts that recorded this information were lost, we are out of luck. We are also at the mercy of the biases of those who wrote the texts that do survive.

- Another discipline that is absolutely essential to understanding the Celts is historical linguistics. This is the study of how languages are related to each other and how they change over time.

- Linguistics, like textual analysis, has its own drawbacks. Languages are very complex. If someone is trying to see relationships between languages, it can be easy to focus on the features that look similar and ignore the differences, or vice-versa, so caution is required.

- Another important academic discipline that is vital to study of the Celts is archaeology, which really developed as an academic discipline starting in the 19th century. Archaeologists work without any texts at all, although of course they are happy to draw on texts when they prove helpful. Their work is focused almost entirely on physical artifacts.

- The drawback of archaeology is the artifacts cannot talk. We cannot be sure from looking at pots or brooches what languages their owners spoke or what ethnic groups they considered themselves to be members of. And we are also limited by what has happened to survive and what archaeologists have happened to find. But a new kind of information may help fill in the gaps: DNA evidence.

Suggested Reading

Caesar, *The Conquest of Gaul*, books 7–8.
Collis, *The Celts*.
Livy, *Early History of Rome*, book 5.
Moody, Martin, and Byrne, *A New History of Ireland*, chapter 4.

Questions to Consider

1. What is the so-called Celtic hypothesis, and does it matter if it turns out to be incorrect?

2. What are the advantages and disadvantages of the different kinds of evidence we can use to learn about the Celts?

Lecture

2

The Celts and the Classical World

This lecture looks at the Celts mostly through the eyes of the Greeks and Romans who wrote about them 2,000-plus ago. We don't have very much information about the ancient Celts that was actually written by the Celts themselves, other than a few mostly fragmentary inscriptions. The reason why is quite interesting. We are told that the druids, who were the intellectuals of the Celtic world, did not believe in writing, reasoning that if people didn't have to make the effort to remember things, then how could they say they really knew them? There was also a trade-secret issue going on. The druids wanted to monopolize sacred lore, but if they wrote it down, perhaps people on the outside could get access to it.

Other reports suggest that the druids did write things down, but that they kept them secret. Thus, almost all of the written texts that we have about the ancient Celts were written by the Greeks and Romans who encountered them. Keep in mind that this lecture mostly discusses how the Celts appeared to outsiders.

Reactions

- Greek and Roman writers had various reactions to the Celts depending on what they were trying to achieve in the different texts they wrote. Sometimes, the Celts appear as barbaric warriors who threaten the survival of classical civilization. Sometimes, they are noble savages whose high ethical standards present a stark contrast with the degraded manners of contemporary Romans. Sometimes, they are merely curiosities exhibited to an interested reading public.

- Another factor to keep in mind is how much these authors actually knew about the Celts. Some of them knew a lot. They actually traveled to the territories where the Celts lived. But other writers had less first-hand knowledge of the people they wrote about, and in some cases, they merely recycled stories they had heard or read elsewhere. Another problem is that many of these texts about the ancient Celts survive only in fragmentary form.

The Name

- An important question is: Where did the name *Celt* come from? There is no easy answer to this question. The word *Celt* was first used by the Greeks to refer to the peoples who lived in Gaul, just north of the Greek colony at Massalia, which is now the French city of Marseilles.

- The earliest author who used the word *Celt* was a man called Hecataeus of Miletus, who described these peoples in 517 BC. We know his work only through extracts that were written down by later authors. The Greeks tended to call these people the *Keltoi* ever after.

- But we don't really know what the word *Celt* refers to. There are various theories. Some linguists think the word means "to hide," but others think it means "to strike" or "to impel." It could mean "foreigners," or it could mean "the tall ones." The Celts were often described as being taller than the Greeks or Romans, so that would fit, but we can't be sure.

- Then we have the problem of what the Romans called the Celts. Some of them just took over the word *Keltoi* from the Greeks and Latinized it as *Celtae*. But most Roman authors referred to these people as *Galli* or *Gauls*. We are not sure if this was originally a name that these people gave to themselves, or perhaps it was a name that a particular tribe gave to itself.

- In the 3rd century, the Greeks called the people who invaded Asia Minor the *Galatae*, which is clearly related to the Galli. This word may have as its root a word that means "warlike," and it may be related to the word that the Irish later used to refer to themselves: the *Gaels*.

- That means there are two different terms for the people this course talks about: the Celts and the Gauls. It is difficult to choose between them or explain their origins very precisely, so for now, the course will use the terms fairly interchangeably. Keep in mind that ancient writers were not necessarily using a consistent definition of the word *Celt* when they used the term.

Writings About the Celts

Herodotus

- We have some very vague indications clustered about the time of Hecataeus of Miletus in the middle of the 1st millennium BC that a people known as the Celts was believed to live in the north and west of Europe. The only thing that is clear about these early references is that these authors did not have the geography very straight at all. For example, the famous Greek historian Herodotus does not seem to be sure whether the Celts live at the source of the Danube River or beyond the Strait of Gibraltar.

- Some travelers ventured into Celtic territory, and we have some tantalizing hints of what they found. For example, we have a very interesting poem called the "Ora Maritima," or "Sea Coasts," which was written in the 4th century AD by a poet named Avienus. The poet claimed that the poem was based the *Massaliote Periplus*, a text from the 6th century BC that lists the major ports and landmarks that a sailor could expect to encounter in the region around Massalia.

The Celtic World | 17

- Fairly early on in the history of writing about the Celts, they got associated with certain traits that stigmatized them as barbarians. Aristotle, for instance, criticized the Celts for having a kind of crazed fearlessness, and he also reported disapprovingly on their predilection for homosexual relationships. (This was an odd criticism, especially given the role of homosexuality in Greek society.)

Aristotle

- Aristotle's teacher Plato criticized the Celts for drunkenness. This cultural habit does seem to have been one of the aspects of Celtic society that classical commentators noticed the most.

- An early writer named Hieronymus of Cardia reports that the Celts lived on the edge of the ocean (presumably meaning the Atlantic Coast) and that they practiced human sacrifice. This is a controversial topic, but shows that the Celts were seen as intimidating and exotic.

- One of the most important writers who talked about the Celts was a man named Poseidonius. He traveled into the heart of Gaul, and he wrote up his findings in a work which, unfortunately, survives only in extracts. The stories he told became a template that other authors referred back to. Julius Caesar, for example, would rely on Poseidonius extensively. He was the first writer to note that the Celts displayed the severed heads of their enemies.

- He also has some of the most extensive information about the fighting techniques of the Celts. Supposedly, they liked to fight naked. Caesar notes that they also treated their hair with a paste made of lime to make it stand up on end, which made them look quite intimidating to their opponents. They also played loud war trumpets, and they were given to challenging their enemies to single combat.

Encounters With the Classical World

- This lecture now turns to three regions where the Celts met up with their classical counterparts: first Italy, then Greece, then Spain. This order roughly reflects the chronology of when the Romans and Greeks went up against the Celts militarily.

- On the Italian Peninsula, Celts were an important presence for as far back as we have written sources to go on. There seem to have been Celtic speakers in northern Italy from very early on. In fact, some of the earliest Celtic inscriptions we have are from northern Italy, from the people we know as the Leponti.

- Other groups of Celtic speakers appeared in northern Italy around 400 BC, likely attracted by the wealth of the Italian Peninsula. They conquered the northern Italian plains (which means that they were conquering other Celtic speakers).

- In 225 BC, a Celtic army was defeated by the Romans at the Battle of Telamon in Tuscany, north of Rome. This was the end of the Celts as an independent power in the north of Italy. From this point on, the Romans spoke of "two Gauls," which were distinguished by their position with respect to the Alps.

- One Gaul was on the Italian side of the Alps. It was called Cisalpine Gaul, from the Latin word *cis*, which means "on this side of." The other Gaul was called Transalpine Gaul, because it was "across," or "on the other side of" the Alps. Cisalpine Gaul was now under Roman domination, but for now, Transalpine Gaul was something the Romans had no interest in reckoning with.

Two Groups

- In the early 3rd century BC, large groups of barbarians swept into Greece from the north. They were taking advantage of the collapse of the empire of Alexander the Great, who had died in 323 BC. In 281 BC, a group of people known to the Greeks as the Galatae and later as the Galatians defeated the Macedonian king Ptolemy. They then split into two main groups.

- One group, under a leader named Brennus, headed south in 279 BC toward the temple at Delphi, which was a tempting target because it functioned as a big bank. Apparently, the Greek gods (especially Pan) intervened to foil the attack by inducing panic among the invaders, who retreated in great disorder. Brennus, in shame, committed suicide.

- The other group headed into central Turkey, where they founded their own state. The Galatians wound up in Turkey by invitation. At that time, present-day Turkey was divided up into many smaller states that were often at war with each other.

- The ruler of one of these states, the kingdom of Bithynia, invited the Galatians in to serve as mercenaries. They didn't manage to defeat the king's enemies, but they did manage to carve out a stronghold for themselves in the interior of Turkey, and they made their living essentially as bandits. They had a very fierce reputation. Various rulers hired them as mercenaries over the years, including people who were resisting the eventual Roman conquest of Turkey.

- The Galatians carried on as a mercenary state down to the time when the Romans conquered the region. In fact, the Galatians backed the Romans against their main opponent, the kingdom of Pontus. As a reward, the Romans allowed the Galatians to maintain their autonomy as a micro-kingdom within Roman-ruled Anatolia.

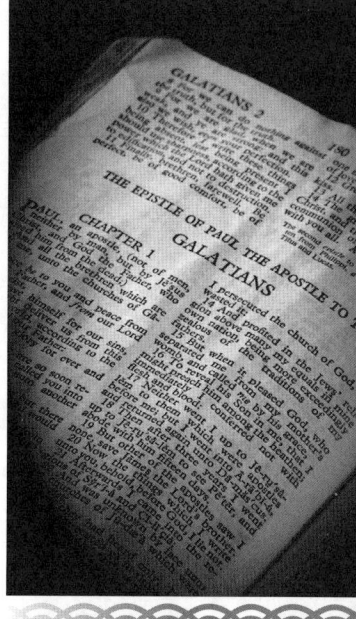

- One group of Galatians eventually came to see a different path and converted to Christianity. These are the Galatians to whom the apostle Paul directed one of his famous epistles. The Galatians were eventually absorbed into the larger Greco-Roman world, but the Galatian language, which was related to Gaulish, survived for hundreds of years thereafter.

The Celts in Spain

- The story of the Celts in Spain (or the Iberian Peninsula) is a very complicated subject. The Romans referred to some of the inhabitants of the Iberian Peninsula as *Celts*, to others as *Iberians*, and to still others as *Celtiberians*, which must mean some kind of mixture of Celtic and Iberian.

The Celtic World | 21

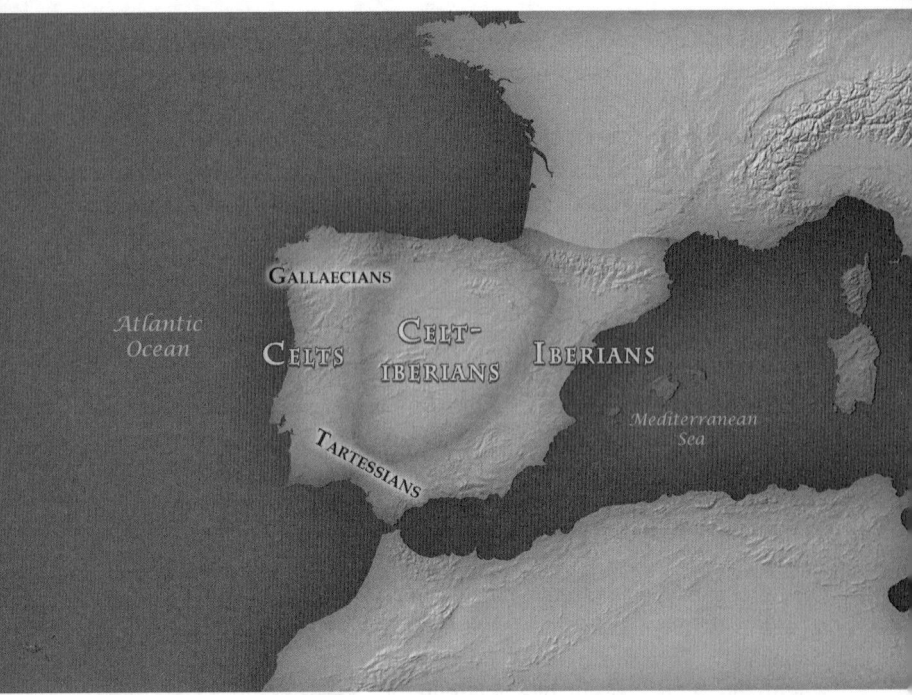

- Charting them is complicated: A relevant map of Iberia is a patchwork, with Celts and Iberians and Celtiberians jumbled up together. There were definitely many Iberians in the middle of the peninsula, and their language was not Celtic.

- We're not even completely sure which of these peoples are Celts. Some scholars are now arguing that the Tartessian language seen in inscriptions that have come to light since the 1990s in southwestern Iberia actually represents an even earlier form of the Celtic language than the Lepontic language found in northern Italy. However, one of the languages spoken in northwestern Spain, Gallaecian, was definitely Celtic.

- The various Celtic groups in Spain, among others, gave the Romans a terrible time. It took well into the 1st century BC before they were entirely subdued.

Suggested Reading

Collis, *The Celts*, chapters 1 and 6.

Freeman, *Ireland and the Classical World*.

———, *The Philosopher and the Druids*.

———, *War, Women, and Druids*.

Koch and Carey, *The Celtic Heroic Age*, pp. 5–39.

Rankin, *Celts and the Classical World*.

Questions to Consider

1. What were some of the aspects of Celtic society that seemed particularly noteworthy to classical authors?

2. How might modern readers need to use classical sources about the Celts with caution?

Lecture

3

Celtic Art and Artifacts

The previous lecture was based very much on written texts. This lecture marks a shift, looking not at written texts but at material objects. We'll see what archaeology can tell us about the Celts. The story is richer but also much more complicated than scholars used to think. A bit of general caution: Ideally, texts and objects will work together to tell a more complete story than either kind of evidence would do all by itself. However, sometimes written texts can be so suggestive that scholars interpret material objects in light of those texts and not on their own terms.

Different Models of Archaeology

- Archaeology has changed in the past half-century or so, but a lot of the earlier models that archaeology started out with have lingered in the popular understanding and even in the work of scholars from other fields. Archaeologists have a tradition of identifying what they call *cultures*, meaning material cultures or artifacts.

- Archaeologists identify cultures based on finding similar artifacts in a particular region, and they usually name them after the most important site where these artifacts were found. However, there are some limitations. Artifacts cannot tell us what language people spoke. They cannot tell us how the people who used those artifacts thought about themselves or what they called themselves. And artifacts have very complicated distribution maps.

- The older model of archaeology helped to create the model of the Celts as a distinct ethnic group that spread out from Central Europe and took over large sections of the European continent. Archaeologists in the 19th century discovered artifacts that they associated with the classical texts about the Celts, and they assumed that the people who owned and used these objects were the same people they read about in the classical texts.

- That model prevailed until the last few decades, and it still exists in popular books and textbooks about the Celts. This course will talk about how that archaeological model for the Celts developed in a later lecture, but this lecture focuses more on what the archaeologists actually found.

The Traditional Story

- The traditional story is that the Celts arose in Central Europe in the middle of the 1st millennium BC in association with two cultures that appeared one after the other, both named for the sites of important archaeological finds. The first site was at Hallstatt in western Austria, and the second site was at La Tène, in western Switzerland.

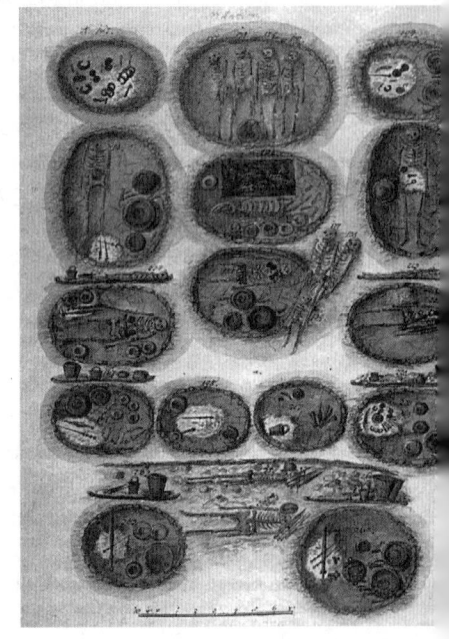

- The Hallstatt culture flourished from roughly 1200 to 475 BC. Starting in the early 19th century, about 1,000 graves were excavated at Hallstatt, dating from the early Iron Age. There were thousands of artifacts in these graves, including weapons and imported Mediterranean vessels. This indicated a flourishing system of long-distance trade.

- Scholars in the 19th century assumed the people buried in the graves were Celts, but we can't be sure. The Hallstatt culture probably actually covered areas that included both Celtic speakers and non-Celtic speakers. Some scholars have proposed a connection between the Celts and the excellent metalwork found in the graves, since the Celts were famous for being excellent metalsmiths.

- That means this was a highly stratified society with far-flung economic ties around Europe and even beyond. That is evident in another very characteristic feature of this period, which is the hillfort. There are dozens of these large fortifications across Central Europe, and they are often associated with princely graves. The hillforts tell us that this society was developing local power centers in which hundreds or even thousands of people could gather.

- At some point around 500–450 BC, the Hallstatt culture seems to have been disrupted, and the hillforts were largely abandoned. New artifacts came in, but we can't be sure whether the Hallstatt people were replaced by entirely new people or whether these were from the descendants of the same people.

- The new culture was named after a site called La Tène in Switzerland, where some of its characteristic artifacts were found. It produced some spectacular art that has become particularly associated with the Celts, though this poses a lot of problems that a later lecture will discuss.

- The La Tène people seem to have traded even more with the Mediterranean than the Hallstatt people, so they must have been even more prosperous and well connected. We can see this from the burial site of a princess found in Vix in eastern France from around 500 BC.

Artifacts

- In the grave was an enormous Greek wine vessel made of bronze. It held 290 gallons, which presupposes a fairly sophisticated social structure, since this princess was not going to drink all that wine by herself. Over 2,500 metal objects were found at the site, most with some military connection. More than 166 swords were found, most of which were never used, indicating ritual functions for the swords.

- Also present were torcs, which are gold neckbands that were worn by both men and women. Many of the torcs were so heavy that they could probably only have been worn by a very large man. Ancient sources often associate torcs with the Celts.

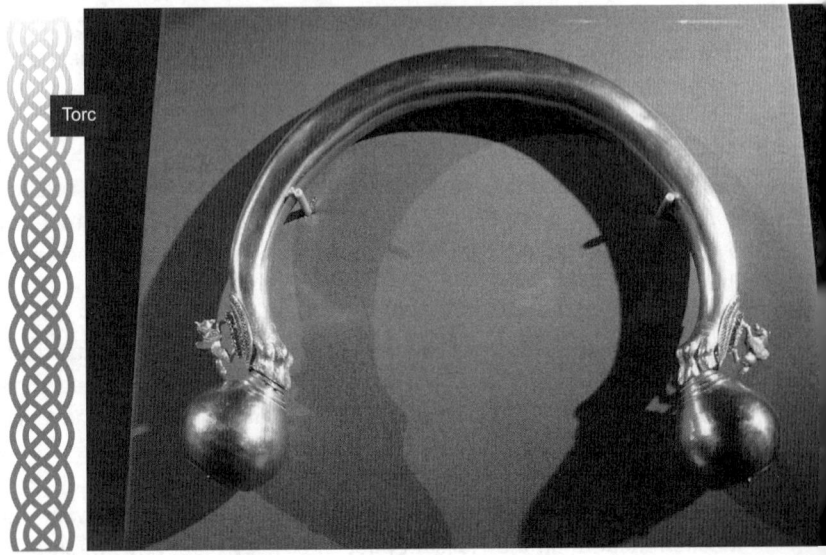
Torc

- Aside from torcs, one of the most interesting artifacts associated with the Celts is a special bronze or copper trumpet called the carnyx, which comes from a Gaulish word meaning "antler" or "horn." The carnyx was a very long tube played vertically. It featured an animal head, often that of a boar. These were used in Celtic military music and produced a loud, aggressive sound.

- Classical sources also mention that carnyces were used in druid ceremonies. Judging from the places they have been found, they certainly seem to have been associated with high status: some have been found in

Carnyx

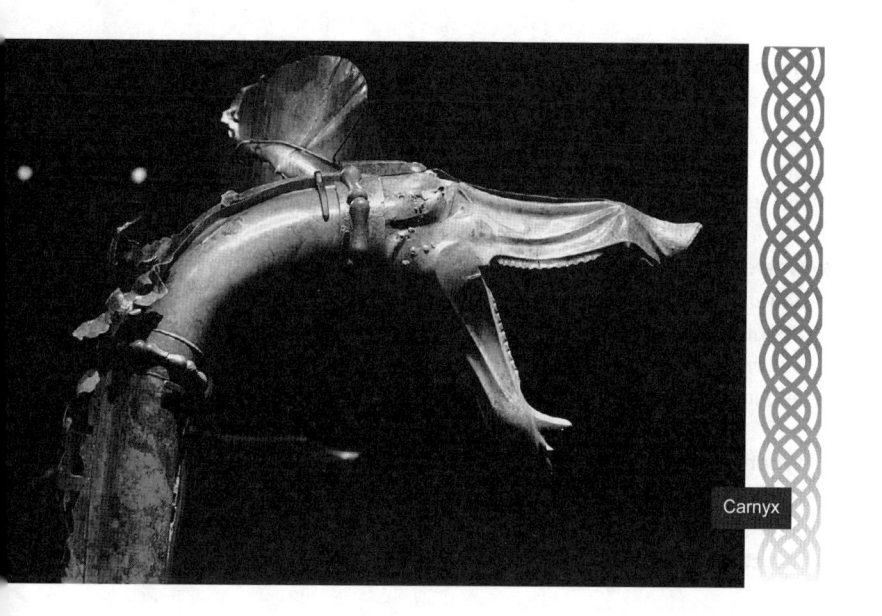

princely graves, and others in places with some sort of ritual function, such as a lake where objects of high prestige were ritually deposited.

- The carnyx was found all over central Europe for a very long period of time, probably from about 300 BC to 300 AD, but the Celts had no monopoly over the carnyx. The instrument was used in regions that were never Celtic speaking, as far as we know, such as northern and southeastern Europe. Torcs, too, were found in areas beyond the Celtic-speaking realm, though it seems as if they had a special significance within Celtic-speaking cultures as a way to denote status.

- Decorative helmets are another artifact associated with the Celts. A highly decorated helmet was an object associated with the elite. These helmets were found all across Europe, and they were often made in the shape of animals. For example, a helmet found at Tintignac was made in the shape of a swan.

Celtic Art

- As their presence on decorative helmets and carnyces indicates, animals play a very important role in Celtic art. Different regions produced different styles. Take, for example, the La Tène style.

- One of this style's most important characteristics is the presence of many spirals and curvilinear forms. This art is all about the curves. But it is also about dense, repeated patterns that look organic and yet are somehow extremely precise. There is an almost modern emphasis on abstraction, and in fact, this art style has proved very influential in modern art.

- When this art does depict figures, they tend to be stylized rather than realistic. It emphasizes the essential elements of figures rather than attempting to capture them in full. There is a persistent fascination with stylistic animal forms.

- One striking aspect of this art as opposed to classical art styles is that we find very few depictions of complete human figures. The human body does not seem to have fascinated these artists the way it did the sculptors and painters of ancient Greece and Rome. One interesting exception is the presence of a number of representations of severed human heads.

The Gundestrup Cauldron

- The famous Gundestrup Cauldron is one of the most impressive masterpieces traditionally associated with the Celts. The story of how it was discovered speaks to the role of chance in archaeology: In 1891 in northern Jutland in Denmark, a laborer digging peat hit something hard with their shovel just before their crew was about to quit for the day.

- The object turned out to be a large silver cauldron containing decorated plates that were stacked inside. These plates would have been fastened to the cauldron both inside and outside. The outer plates depict various

The Gundestrup Cauldron

human-like figures who appear to be gods, since they are engaged in superhuman feats. The inner plates depict more complicated scenes of military life and hunting, including the image of the carnyx. The best recent estimate of its age is that it dates to around 150–50 BC.

- The Gundestrup Cauldron is highly controversial. The controversy over the cauldron very neatly sums up the contrast between the old view of the Celts as a distinct people with a consistent cultural identity and the new view of the Celts as a more fluid grouping of peoples who were open to many influences.

- In the past, the Gundestrup Cauldron has always been classified as a Celtic object, mostly because the assumption is that the people who lived in this part of Europe had to have been Celts. But many aspects of the cauldron do not seem Celtic at all. For example, it has none of the abstract patterning that is so characteristic of the La Tène style.

- Another question is what the figures on the cauldron represent. One notable feature of the cauldron is the fact that unlike a lot of other artifacts made in the so-called Celtic style, it does have a number of human portraits. Those who want to read the cauldron as a so-called Celtic object see Celtic gods and mythological figures.

- The most famous of these figures is a man with antlers who has been identified as the Celtic god of the hunt, Cernunnos. But not everyone sees these figures as Celtic gods. Some art historians who look at the cauldron see more Mediterranean influences or even central Asian elements in the figures.

- People in Central Europe were in contact with all those places, so it's possible that European craftsmen simply took motifs that they had come across and made them their own. We can't be sure if the people who made it were Celts, but its presence all the way in Denmark testifies to the sophistication of the society that produced it and valued it.

Suggested Reading

Collis, *The Celts*, chapters 5–8.

Farley and Hunter, *Celts*, chapters 1–5.

Megaw and Megaw, *Celtic Art*.

"The Hochford/Enz Celtic Museum: A Find of the Century and Its Museum," Keltenmuseum Hochdorf/Enz, http://www.keltenmuseum.de/English/.

Questions to Consider

1. How do changes in archaeologists' views of culture affect our understanding of the Celts?

2. What can Celtic artifacts tell us about the relationships between the people of central Europe and the wider world?

Lecture 4

Celtic Languages in the Ancient World

This lecture covers another kind of information that scholars use to reconstruct the world of the Celts: language. The scholars who work on this field are called linguists or historical linguists. Historical linguistics is one of the most important fields of study for understanding the Celts because languages preserve all kinds of essential information about the people who spoke them.

But language must be used with extreme caution. Just as we are no longer sure that using a particular kind of artifact made someone a Celt, we cannot be sure that people who spoke a certain language identified themselves in a particular way unless we have corroborating evidence that they did so. With that caution in mind, we need to embrace historical linguistics, because while language does not tell the whole story, it tells a large part of it.

Origins

- Linguistic evidence complicates the old picture of the Celts arising in Central Europe around Hallstatt and La Tène. That model argues that the Celtic languages arose in central Europe thousands of years ago among the ancestors of the peoples who produced princely artifacts at Hochdorf.

- The old model of a unified Celtic origin and Celtic identity needs the Celtic languages to start out in the same place as the Celtic art and artifacts associated with the Celts. Otherwise, the claim that one specific group is responsible for all the traits that we associate with being Celtic falls apart.

- The Celtic languages are a branch of the Indo-European family of languages. The Indo-European languages include most of the languages spoken in Europe today, as well as many of the languages spoken in the Middle East and the Indian subcontinent. These languages all derive from a common ancestor many thousands of years ago.

- Scholars are not sure exactly when or where these languages appeared, but the best estimate at the moment is that they developed somewhere in the Caucasus region of west-central Asia, perhaps around 6000 BC. By around 3500 BC, it is clear that branches of the Indo-European family had begun to diverge.

- Linguists believe that at some point, perhaps around 3000 BC (though there some debate), a language broke off from the main Indo-European family that we can call proto-Celtic, or early Celtic. That language would develop into the specific Celtic languages that we know today. The problem is that we are not exactly sure where Celtic fits on the family tree of Indo-European. What are its closest neighbors? What Indo-European languages is it most similar to?

- If we can find what language group Celtic is the most similar to, and if we know where that language group comes from, perhaps can find out where Celtic comes from. It used to be thought that the Celtic languages were most similar to the Italic languages. These are the languages spoken in Italy, so Latin would be the most famous Italic language, though there are many others. This idea is called the Italo-Celtic hypothesis.

- However, there is a problem. Celtic is less similar to Italic than scholars originally thought. There are similarities in vocabulary, but they probably come from two different sources, neither of which argues for a close relationship between Celtic and Italic.

- The similarities date so far back that they don't tell us anything very specific about the relationship between Celtic and Italic. Additionally, there are vocabulary words that have probably been borrowed very recently from one language into the other. The borrowing was too recent for them to demonstrate that the languages are closely related on a fundamental level.

Words

- The kinds of words that were borrowed from the Celtic language can tell us something about what the Romans found striking about the Celts. In many cases, the words they borrowed represented concepts or artifacts that were new to the Romans.

- One example is the word *bracae*, which was borrowed into Latin from Celtic. It means "trousers" or "pants." The word has a distant Germanic origin; the Celtic-speakers themselves borrowed it from the Germans and transmitted it to the Romans. That means this word cannot help us prove a close relationship between Italic and Celtic.

- Other words that the Romans borrowed from Celtic tell us that the Romans were very struck by Celtic customs with regard to war and religion. The Romans borrowed a Celtic word for "javelin" (*gaesa*) and another for "chariot" (*essedum*). They borrowed words for "bard" and "druid," and we still use those words in English today. They also borrowed a word for beer (*cervesia*). Keep in mind that the Romans were wine drinkers. Beer was something of a novelty to them, just like pants.

A New Model

- A new model has arisen recently that tries to account for the rise of the Celtic languages in a totally different way. This is the so-called Celtic from the west model. The idea is that Celtic took shape as a language group not in Central Europe but on the western, Atlantic coast of Europe.

- This theory is based on the fact that there are a lot of similarities in the material remains of the peoples who lived on the west coast of Europe dating back to the Bronze Age. These remains include the great stone monuments known as megaliths, which we see in western Spain, western France, Britain, and Ireland. The most famous of these is undoubtedly Stonehenge, but there are thousands of others.

- The assumption behind this theory is that people who produce similar artifacts and trade with each other across a wide geographical area must have had a means to communicate with each other. Perhaps this means of communication was a proto-Celtic language. Note that it cannot be proven, but it does have its supporters. A famous British archaeologist named Colin Renfrew proposed the theory. Many of the people who like this theory are also archaeologists.

Relations

- Another question regarding about the various Celtic languages is how they relate to each other. Again, we have an old model and a newer model to consider here.

- The traditional way to think about the Celtic languages is to divide them into two main groups: continental Celtic languages and insular Celtic languages—that is, languages spoken on the continent of Europe and languages spoken in the British Isles and Ireland.

- The insular languages are then further broken down into two main groups called Goidelic and Brythonic. Goidelic refers to the Gaelic languages, which include Irish Gaelic, Scottish Gaelic, and Manx, the language of the Isle of Man. Brythonic refers to the languages that were historically spoken on the island of Britain that now include Welsh and Cornish, but also Breton, which is now spoken in Brittany by the descendants of immigrants from Britain, who arrived in western France in the 5th century.

- The two main branches of Celtic are quite similar to each other, but there are also some key differences that make it easy to tell one branch apart from the other. The most obvious way in which they are different is in their handling of the /p/ sound. All Celtic languages lost the /p/ sound at some point in the remote Celtic past. The Goidelic languages mostly never regained the /p/ whereas the Brittonic languages got it back much later.

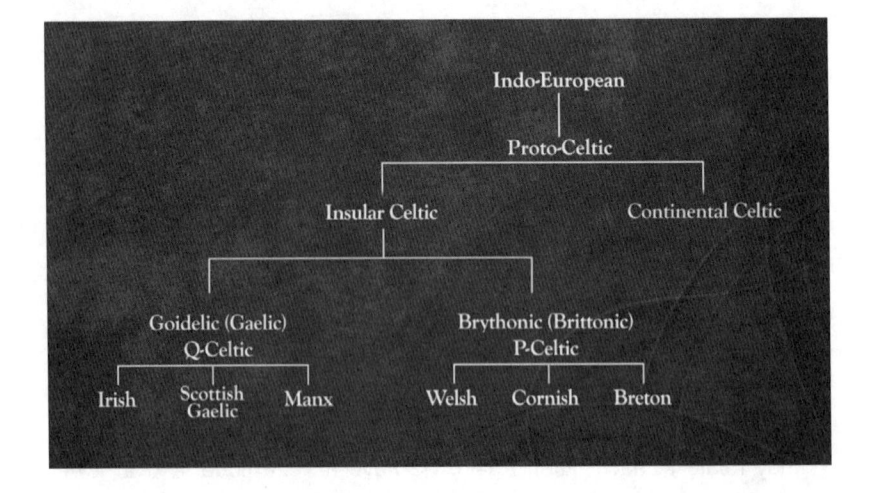

```
                        Indo-European
                             |
                        Proto-Celtic
          ┌──────────────────┴──────────────────┐
     Insular Celtic                      Continental Celtic
          |
  ┌───────┴────────┐
 Goidelic (Gaelic)          Brythonic (Brittonic)
    Q-Celtic                       P-Celtic
 ┌────┬────┐              ┌────────┬────────┐
Irish Scottish Manx      Welsh  Cornish   Breton
      Gaelic
```

- There are many cases in which a Welsh word will have a p, but the Irish word will instead have a /k/ sound spelled with a c. We refer to this as Q-Celtic because the letter q is actually supposed to represent the sound made by a k plus a w. The other part of the living Celtic language family is known as P-Celtic.

- Q-Celtic languages are spoken in Ireland, in northern Britain, and on the Isle of Man in the Irish Sea. The P-Celtic languages are spoken in western Britain, southwestern Britain, and western France. We can account for the presence of Q-Celtic in northern Britain because we know from the historical record that Irish settlers brought the Irish language to what is now Scotland.

- Speakers of P-Celtic took their language to Brittany. Otherwise, it is very clear that Q-Celtic is an Irish phenomenon, and P-Celtic is associated with the island of Britain. Scholars used to account for this division by matching up the linguistic map with the traditional view of how the Celts had arrived in the British Isles and Ireland.

- It used to be thought that the Celts invaded Britain and Ireland from Gaul in the centuries before Christ, and brought the whole Celtic toolkit with them: language, art, and so on. But if so, how are we to account for the fact that Celtic came in these two big varieties, P-Celtic and Q-Celtic?

A Theory of Invasions

- The solution that scholars came up with was to propose that there had been two different Celtic invasions, one by Q-Celtic speakers and one by P-Celtic speakers. Q-Celtic looks more archaic to linguists for various reasons, so the idea was that an initial wave of invaders crossed from the continent into Britain and into Ireland, where they conquered the previous inhabitants and then settled down to speak their P-Celtic language.

- Several centuries later, a second wave of Celtics, this time P-Celtic speakers, invaded the island of Britain, but never made it as far as Ireland. They simply conquered any Q-Celtic speakers in Britain who hadn't made it all the way to Ireland, plus any of the indigenous inhabitants of Britain who were left. Thus, P-Celtic prevailed in Britain, while Q-Celtic continued to be spoken in Ireland.

- The problem with this theory is that there is no evidence for it whatsoever. There doesn't seem to have been any invasion. The people in Britain and Ireland were probably speaking Celtic languages for hundreds if not thousands of years before Christ, and we still aren't really sure how or why the Celtic languages got there.

- All we can really say at this point is that the old model of Celtic spreading out of Hallstatt in central Europe is probably wrong, and that the whole picture is much more complicated than we used to think.

Characteristics of Celtic Languages

- Though we can't be sure of the origin of Celtic languages, we can discuss some of their most striking characteristics. One is the previously mentioned loss of the Indo-European /p/ sound, which Welsh later got back.

- Another notable characteristic is the absence in Celtic of the verb *to have*. In Celtic, speakers use the verb *to be* and a preposition. Things are literally "at" the person who possessed them. A quick example: If someone wanted to say "I have a couple of words of Irish," meaning, "I speak only a little bit of Irish," they would say in Irish: "*Ta cupla focail Gaeilge agam.*" This literally means: "A few words of Irish are at me."

- The most distinctive feature of the Celtic languages by far is called initial mutation. This means that words in the Celtic languages can change their beginning sound based on the properties of the word that comes before them.

Conclusion

- What light can the Celtic languages shed on the problem of Celtic origins and identity? So far, the picture is more complicated than we used to think, and thus more fascinating. Celtic may have arisen in Western Europe rather than in Central Europe, as scholars used to think, but it's also possible that Celtic underwent some mysterious developments in the remote past that brought Celtic speakers into contact with peoples in almost every corner of the Indo-European world.

- Celtic words were borrowed into Latin, and that tells us that the Celts and the Romans were very familiar with each other's culture. And we can guess that the divisions between the modern Celtic languages preserve some record of the different ways in which Celtic made its way to Britain and Ireland.

- Beyond that, we have the languages themselves, in all their complexity. In future lectures we will look at the literature of the Celtic languages in detail, because if we can be certain of anything about the Celts, it is the fact that language and literature were central to their society.

Suggested Reading

Ball and Müller, *The Celtic Languages*, parts 1–3.

Collis, *The Celts*, chapter 3.

Cunliffe and Koch, *Celtic from the West*, part 3.

———, *Celtic from the West 2*, chapter 8.

Macaulay, *The Celtic Languages*.

Renfrew, "Ethnogenesis."

Russell, *An Introduction to the Celtic Languages*.

Questions to Consider

1. How do different theories about the origins of the Celtic languages complicate our picture of the Celts?

2. What are the most important characteristics of the Celtic languages?

Lecture 5

Caesar and the Gauls

This lecture concentrates on a very specific, very important encounter between the Celts and the classical world. The lecture looks at the process by which Rome finally conquered and assimilated the Gaulish territory in both northern Italy and what is now France, and it focuses particularly on Julius Caesar's famous conquest of Gaul. We will see that the Celts often got drawn into the larger story of the slow but inexorable growth of Roman power in the western Mediterranean.

Politics

- In contrast to the raids by the Celts on Italy and Greece, Caesar's campaigns in Gaul targeted the homeland of the Celts themselves. The story of why Caesar went into Gaul involves political intrigue on both the Roman side and the Gaulish side.

- The story starts in the mid-3rd century BC, not in Gaul but in northern Italy, which was a Celtic-speaking area. After the clashes between the Gauls and the Romans in the 4th century BC, the Romans had pushed back against the Gauls living in northern Italy. This was in the Po Valley, a region that they called Cisalpine Gaul.

- By the 220s BC, the Romans had thoroughly militarized this region. They had imposed Roman garrisons on the population, and they were planting colonies of Romans among the native Celts, whose most important tribe was called the Boii.

- The Boii were not giving up just yet. They allied with Hannibal, the famous Carthaginian commander, against the Romans. Celtic warriors proved indispensible to him. They played a role in helping him reach the Po Valley, win battles, and in Rome's greatest military defeat at the Battle of Cannae.

Hannibal

- Hannibal eventually lost the war, but the close alliance between the northern Italian Celts and Rome's fiercest opponent did not endear the Celts to the Romans. Rome spent the next several decades systematically conquering the Celtic territory of northern Italy and Romanizing any of the Celts who were not driven across the Alps.

- By the end of the 1st century BC, the former Cisalpine Gaul was just part of Italy. (However, the Celts of this area did play a role in the 73 BC slave revolt led by Spartacus, marking them as an ally of another of Rome's enemies.) The Transalpine Gaul area did not assimilate.

Massalia

- A land route between Italy and Spain was crucial to the Romans if they wanted to keep in contact with their colonies in Spain. Right in the middle of this land route was the city of Massalia, a Greek colony founded in 600 BC that would become the modern city of Marseilles.

- In the middle of the 2nd century BC, Massalia was attacked by a tribe known as the Salyes, which were referred to by Roman sources as Celto-Ligurians, which means that the Romans were actually confused about the identity of these people. Massalia called on Rome for help.

- Rome took the opportunity to make a deal with Massalia: Rome would help against Massalia's enemies, but in return, they wanted to annex their hinterland. Massalia said yes, and Rome then defeated some of the Celtic allies of the Salyes to the north of Massalia. Rome thereby acquired an important strip of coastal territory in Gaul that they named simply the Province, which is the origin of the modern French name of the region: Provence.

Instability

- In Gaul, various Celtic tribes jockeyed for supremacy. One tribe in particular, the Cimbri, became a threat to Rome around 113 BC. They appeared in the Rhône Valley, just north of Massalia, in the territory that the Romans now considered their own backyard, and began stirring up trouble.

- The Cimbri allied with other tribes, including the Teutones. Over the course of less than a decade, various Gaulish tribes defeated four large Roman armies sent to contain them. By 105 BC, there was nothing between the Gaulish armies and Rome itself.

- But instead of heading for Rome, the Cimbri and Teutones turned around and headed west for Iberia, where they plundered for a while before being driven out in turn by the Celtiberians. The Romans had been lucky, but it would be easy to see why Gaul was considered a threat to the security of the empire.

- In 102 BC, a group of Teutones and another tribe called the Ambrones moved south to threaten the Po Valley. The Roman commander was Gaius Marius, who is most famous today for having reorganized the Roman army into a professional fighting force. Marius drove the Teutones and Ambrones back up into Gaul and caught them near Aix, where he encircled them and slaughtered them.

- For a few generations after Marius's success, there was relative peace in Gaul, but things were still far from stable. Starting in the mid-60s BC, Gaul began to be threatened by new invaders from the north and east, namely various tribes of Germans. The inhabitants of Gaul began remilitarizing in response.

- In particular, the various tribal federations reoccupied the large hillforts that had characterized the area hundreds of years earlier. We know these fortresses by the Latin word *oppida*; the singular is *oppidum*. An oppidum was basically a glorified hillfort, but these oppida were very strong militarily; often walls of stone or timber and extensive earthworks defended them.

Gaius Marius

Caesar

- The story of the Roman conquest of Gaul demonstrates not that the Celtic tribes were barbaric but rather that they were not all that different from their neighbors to the south, despite what Caesar might have wanted the readers of his work, *Commentaries on the Gallic War*, to believe. Regardless, Caesar's work shows much about the wars Caesar fought against the Gauls.

- In the middle of the 1st century BC, the Celtic-speaking tribes in Gaul had consolidated themselves into several major coalitions. Caesar tells us that Gaul was divided into three parts: Aquitania in the southwest (which is where we get the later name Aquitaine from), Belgica in the north (the origin of the name Belgium), and Celtica, which was essentially what is now central and southeastern France. The main events that touched off the conquest happened in the Celtica region.

- In many ways, the Roman conquest of Gaul was an accident, and it involved serious political rivalries within the ruling elites of both Rome and Gaul. Two of the most important tribal groupings in Celtica were the Sequani, who lived on the western bank of the Rhine, and the Aedui, who lived just to the west of them, in what is now central France.

- In 71 BC, the Sequani and the Aedui got involved in a quarrel. The Sequani needed some help. They decided to call in their neighbors from the eastern bank of the Rhine, a Germanic tribe called the Suebi, led by a chieftain called Ariovistus. After they defeated the Aedui, the Suebi stuck around and began exacting tribute from the Celtic tribes in the vicinity.

- The Aedui decided to look for allies of their own, and the most powerful people they could think of to call on were the Romans. In 60 BC, the chieftain of the Aedui, a man named Divitiacos, appealed to Rome for help against the Germans.

- When Divitiacos visited Rome, he was the guest of Cicero's younger brother, and Cicero himself mentions Divitiacos in his letters. Divitiacos addressed the Roman Senate to ask for an alliance. He returned to Gaul with some a vague promise of Roman help, and Cicero certainly backed the idea of an alliance with the Aedui.

Julius Caesar

Cicero

- But Roman politics did not break in a way that favored the Gauls. Cicero's most dangerous political opponent was Julius Caesar, a rising star who became consul in 59 BC. He decided that instead of backing an alliance with the Aedui under Divitiacos, Rome should make an alliance with the Germans under Ariovistus. The fact that Julius Caesar was on the German side just made the Suebi even bolder, and they made even more inroads into Celtic territory.

- By this point, the various tribes of Gaul were split internally over whether it made sense to accommodate themselves to outside domination, whether by Romans or by Germans. Many tribal leaders, like Divitiacos of the Aedui, thought this was the best bet they had. But the younger brother of Divitiacos, a man called Dumnorix, thought that cozying up to the Romans was getting them nowhere.

- He put out feelers to his father-in-law Orgetorix, the chieftain of the Helvetii, who were a large Celtic tribe that occupies the territory now known as Switzerland. Orgetorix also made an alliance with the disaffected son of the chieftain of the Sequani, a man named Casticos. The idea of this alliance was to bring together all the Celts in one united federation to resist encroachment by either the Germans or the Romans.

Roman Machinations

- In 60 BC, Julius Caesar entered into a pact with two other powerful Roman political figures, Pompey the Great and Crassus. This alliance was called the First Triumvirate. The alliance was not founded on mutual respect, however, but on the recognition that none of the three was (yet) powerful enough to do in the others.

- The three men carved up the Roman Empire into spheres of influence. Caesar got the provinces of Illyricum, Cisalpine Gaul, and Gallia Narbonensis, which was another name for the Province, or Provence. These were not the richest parts of the empire. Pompey and Crassus got those. If Caesar was going to make a profit, both economically and politically, he was going to need to expand the territory under his command. That meant expanding into Gaul.

- In 58 BC, Caesar got the perfect excuse, when the Celtic world suddenly became even more unstable than usual. Several Germanic tribes began moving into the territory of the Helvetii from the north and the northeast, and the Helvetii decided to move west to get out of their way. By this point, their chieftain, Orgetorix, had died.

- This migration was not a panicked flight, but a rather orderly mass movement, made possible by an alliance between Dumnorix of the Aedui and Casticos of the Sequani. The Helvetii made arrangements with both men to let them pass through their respective territories to settle to their west in Gaul.

- Keep in mind that Dumnorix and Casticos were not calling the shots for the Aedui and the Sequani. The chieftain of the Aedui, Divitiacos, was pro-Roman; he had made a speech to the Senate to ask for a Roman alliance.

- Despite the fact that Julius Caesar had not been interested in a Roman alliance with the Aedui a few years earlier, Divitiacos was willing to give it another shot. He sent word to Caesar that the Helvetii were on the move. Caesar was eager to demonstrate to the other two members of the Triumvirate, as well as the Roman population at large, that he was fully capable of protecting his province of Gallia Narbonensis from these migrating Gauls.

- Caesar marched north to meet the Helvetii. They turned northwest into the territory of the Aedui, and Caesar followed. The arrival of Caesar blew open the tensions among the Aedui between pro-Roman and anti-Roman factions.

- Many of the Aedui were giving aid to the Helvetii. Caesar demanded that they cease and desist, and he probably called for the capture and elimination of Divitiacos's anti-Roman brother, Dumnorix. But Divitiacos did not give his brother up.

- Despite the failure of Divitiacos to cooperate, Caesar went after the Helvetii and caught them. In a series of battles, he massacred huge numbers. Of the 400,000 members of the Helvetii who began their migration, only a quarter survived, and these survivors were forced to go back to their homeland. Incoming Germanic tribes eventually overran them, and their language died out.

- Caesar's demonstration of ruthlessness led some of the other tribes in Gaul to decide that making peace with Caesar was by far the best option, and they figured that if they did so, Caesar might help them against Ariovistus and his Germans.

- Caesar challenged Ariovistus, who defied him. Ariovistus began gathering his forces in the territory of the Sequani, who were anti-Roman

Celts. Caesar went after Ariovistus and destroyed his army. There was now nobody else for the Romans to compete against in Gaul.

- The following year, 57 BC, Caesar moved north to campaign against the Belgae, who were the least Romanized of the Gauls. He carried out a brutal campaign of sieges and slaughter. The year after that, Caesar conquered the Veneti, a seafaring people who lived on the Armorican peninsula, in what is now Brittany.

- He then defeated another attempted German incursion into Gaul. Caesar reports himself that of 430,000 members of the tribe, only a few survived. And when he finished with the Germans, Caesar undertook two extended raids into the island of Britain, in 55 and 54 BC.

Revolt

- A major revolt in 54–52 BC nearly undid Caesar's accomplishments. In 54 BC, the political winds shifted throughout Gaul in favor of the anti-Roman party. Almost the whole of Gaul rose in rebellion, led by a chieftain of the Treveri tribe, a man named Indutiomaros. Caesar's response was to put a price on Indutiomaros's head. Indutiomaros was ambushed and killed by a Gaulish traitor. After several other brutal campaigns in 53 BC, Caesar reestablished control sufficiently to withdraw from Gaul for the winter.

- But the Gauls were not yet cowed. Caesar found a worthy opponent in a man named Vercingetorix, who was named the chieftain of the Arverni tribe in 52 BC. The Arverni controlled the territory in south central France near what is now Clermont-Ferrand. As soon as Vercingetorix took power, he set about creating an alliance to resist Roman rule.

- He went up against Caesar at the Battle of Gergovia, the chief oppidum of the Arverni. Vercingetorix defeated Caesar, one of the only times Caesar was ever defeated in battle. This victory put heart into the Gaulish resistance, but ultimately, Caesar prevailed.

- The last stand of Vercingetorix was very dramatic. He holed up in the fortress of Alesia near Dijon in north central France. Caesar decided to besiege him in Alesia. Vercingetorix called on his Gaulish allies to come and surround Caesar. But Caesar built a fortress of his own facing out towards the armies that might come to relieve Alesia.

- Although the Gaulish allies who arrived to help were not as numerous as Vercingetorix might have hoped, they were still able to spot a weakness in Caesar's fortifications. When the Gaulish allies on the outside combined with Vercingetorix's forces on the inside, they nearly squeezed Caesar between them and defeated him.

- Caesar personally took command of the very last reserves he had available to them and pulled out a victory. Keep in mind that we know all of this from Caesar's own pen—it's possible that he is making these events sound a bit more dramatic than they actually were.

- Vercingetorix was taken off to captivity in Rome, until it was finally time for Caesar's triumph to be celebrated six years later. Vercingetorix was paraded through the streets of Rome, where he presumably had to put up with the jeers and other abuse of the crowd, and then returned to his prison, where he was probably strangled, as was the custom with the defeated enemies of the Romans. Thus ended the last major rebel against Roman rule in Gaul.

Consequences

- Roman culture quickly became widespread throughout Gaul, at least in the areas that were within easy distance of Roman settlements, and also all along the Roman road network. There, the Latin language came into very wide use, and all the trappings of Roman civilization followed the legions.

- But we have evidence that the Gaulish language persisted. The evidence comes from a remarkable artifact known as the Coligny Calendar, which was made in the 2nd century AD. The labels on the calendar are in the Gaulish language, but in the Roman alphabet.

- The existence of this calendar is evidence of the survival not just of the Gaulish language but also of this very important aspect of Gaulish culture: the reckoning of time. Utimately, Gaulish did fade away, but it left some traces in the French language that is descended from the Latin that replaced it.

- It had been very hard fought, but the Gauls were now firmly under Roman rule. The last remaining areas of Celtic speech outside of the Roman Empire were Britain and Ireland.

Suggested Reading

Caesar, *The Conquest of Gaul*.
Ellis, *The Celtic Empire*.

Questions to Consider

1. How did political tensions both within the Celtic world and within the Roman world contribute to Caesar's conquest of Gaul?

2. Does the story of Caesar's conquest support or undermine the classical picture of the Celts as so-called barbarians?

Lecture

6

Celtic Religion and the Druids

This lecture focuses on religion and the Celts, and particularly the role of druids in Celtic society. The lecture looks at the general beliefs of the Celtic peoples, insofar as we can access them, and then talks about druids in some detail. However, part of the problem with reconstructing pagan religion is that we have two kinds of texts about the topic that we might use, but each of these kinds of texts has drawbacks. The first type of text is reports about the Celts by the Romans and Greeks; we can't be sure how well these writers understood their subject, but we need to make the best of them.

The other kind of text was at least written by people we think of now as Celts, especially the Irish, but there are two problems with these texts. The first is that they were all written down after the Irish converted to Christianity, so people were looking back on beliefs that they no longer held. The second problem is that we are not entirely sure how much of a connection there is between the people of Ireland, for example, and the people of Gaul. However, there are at least some intriguing parallels that could make us inclined to accept a connection between different areas of the Celtic-speaking world.

Views on the Celtic Pantheon

- Celtic mythology is hard to reconstruct, but it seems to have focused on a pantheon of nature-related gods and also belief in an Otherworld that was located either across the sea or under the ground. But when we start to get specific, the picture is murkier. It is hard if not impossible to reconstruct anything like a unified Celtic pantheon that stretches across all the Celtic lands.

- One of the aspects of Celtic belief that struck the classical authors the most forcefully was their fixation with treasure, especially gold, which was often offered as a sacrifice to their gods. For instance, we have several reports of how the Gauls would deposit large amounts of gold and silver in their temples, and the Greek historian Strabo reports in amazement that the treasure would be absolutely safe; nobody would think of touching it.

- But according to another Greek historian, Poseidonius, besides offering treasure as a sacrifice in temples, the Gauls would deposit gold and silver in lakes. The Celts believed in an Otherworld for which water was a kind of boundary, so by depositing the treasure in lakes, they were essentially sending it to the realm of the gods.

- Strabo tells us that whenever a Gaulish region was conquered, the Roman authorities would auction off these lakes to raise money for the public treasury. Presumably, the buyers of the lakes would then drain them (it helped that the Romans were excellent engineers) and then scoop up all the treasure at the bottom.

- We have evidence that the Celts had some kind mystical connection to birds. A historian from the late 3rd century BC named Eudoxus reported that if the plagues of locusts descended on the crops of the Celts, the Celts would use special prayers and offer special sacrifices to attract flocks of birds, who would come and eat the locusts.

- There are also signs that the Celts attached some kind of religious or at least symbolic significance to the severed human head. The Roman historian Livy recorded a story about what happened to the Roman general Postumius when he was killed while fighting against the Boii tribe of Cisalpine Gaul in northern Italy.

Livy

- According to Livy, the Gauls took his severed head in a procession to their chief temple, and once the skull had been cleaned, they ornamented it with gold and used it thereafter as a drinking cup for their priests on special occasions. (This story should be approached with caution, because Livy was writing two centuries after the fact, and we also have reports of other ancient peoples using skulls as cups.)

- One of the Celtic beliefs that caused the most comment among ancient writers was the belief in reincarnation, which was incidentally a belief that the famous Greek philosopher Pythagoras shared. The historian Diodorus reports that the Gauls believed that a few years after death, a departed person would be reborn into a new body. He states that some Gauls would throw letters into a funeral pyre so that people who had already died could read them.

Druids

- Druids were important figures in Celtic religion. Druids seem to have been a feature of British, Irish, and Gaulish society, but they are not found in every part of Europe where Celtic languages were spoken. Druids were apparently especially popular in Britain

- Caesar reports that the druids were extremely powerful in Gaulish society. In fact, he put the druids on an equal footing with warriors in the social pecking order in Gaul. The druids were essentially the intelligentsias. They controlled religious life, but they were also the lawyers and judges of the Gauls.

- The high social status of druids put them at the center of politics in Celtic territories. Druids were often seen as the heart of Celtic resistance to Roman authority. Julius Caesar worried about druids during his conquest of

Gaul, and when the Romans conquered Britain, one of their top priorities was to destroy the druid center on the island of Mona.

- But if the Romans feared druids, they were also fascinated by them. For some very interesting details about druids, we can turn to the *Natural History* by the Roman author Pliny the Elder. Pliny reports that the druids worshiped only in oak groves and would not carry out their ceremonies unless a branch of that tree is present.

- Druids trained for many years to master very complex texts by memory, since they did not believe in writing down sacred things. It could take as long as 20 years to become a fully trained druid. We can be fairly sure that the druids had a belief in fate, or at least in luck, in the sense that some times were lucky while others were unlucky.

- The Coligny Calendar artifact seems to provide confirmation that druids were in charge of determining which days were auspicious for engaging in certain activities. For example, Poseidonius tells us that the druids were often in charge of deciding whether it was a good day to give battle.

A High Cost

- Knowledge of the future and of what days were lucky came at a high cost. We have many early references to the Celts practicing human sacrifice. The earliest, very fragmentary reference to Celtic human sacrifice comes from a Greek comic tirade written in the late 4th century BC, in which the author, Sopater, is denouncing three fellow writers. He tells his audience that he would like to do to these terrible writers what the Celts do to their enemies after a successful battle—that is, "sacrifice their prisoners to the gods."

- Poseidonius tells us that the Gaulish druids would use human victims to foretell the future. The druids would stab a man right above his diaphragm, and then, "When the man has collapsed from the wound, they interpret the future by observing the nature of his fall, the convulsion of his limbs, and especially from the pattern of his spurting blood."

- Julius Caesar reports that the druids would build enormous figures in which they would encase their victims and then set them alight. But human sacrifice apparently came in various forms—that is, there were different ways in which the victims might be sacrificed.

- We might even have direct evidence of one of the alternatives to burning people alive, since many bodies of people who were ritually killed have been recovered from bogs in Celtic territory. (Note that the practice of burying people in bogs seems to have been widespread across northern Europe, whether the land was ever inhabited by Celtic speakers or not.)

Female Druids

- We have reports that some druids were women. They were probably small in number, but they were not unknown. The classical sources note the presence of women druids, and they crop up in later Irish literature as well.

- For example, in Poseidonius's work, there is a report of an island in the Atlantic Ocean that was inhabited entirely by women who worshiped in the cult of Dionysus. (Dionysus is the Greek god of wine; it's likely Poseidonius was engaging in the well-known classical practice of equating any gods he came across among foreigners with gods he was familiar from in his own pantheon).

- Supposedly, these women would come to the mainland once a year to sleep with men, and then they would return to the island. They would also engage in a bizarre ritual every year by which they would take the roof off a temple piece by piece and then build it back up again, and if any of the women dropped her load, the others would tear her to pieces.

- Poseidonius even tells us that the fix was in: A specific woman was bumped by the others to make her drop her load. It's a very puzzling account, but at the very least, it's an indication of the kinds of things that classical writers believed about the Celts.

The Calendar

- There are clues in the way the Celts organized time that they probably believed in some sort of pantheon of gods that was connected to the natural world. There are some intriguing parallels between the Coligny Calendar of 2nd-century Gaul and the system of reckoning time that we can observe a few centuries later in Ireland. For example, in both Ireland and Gaul, the week was reckoned to be eight days long, and the day was reckoned to last from sundown to sundown, unlike the Roman system, which reckoned the day from sunrise to sunrise.

- The Coligny Calendar does not tell us about how the seasons worked in Gaul, but in Ireland, the calendar was organized around the four main turning points of the agricultural year. These turning points are exactly six weeks off from the turning points we recognize under our modern calendar, which was based on the Roman calendar.

- Our calendar recognizes the changes of the seasons by noting the two solstices and the two equinoxes, that is, the days when the day is longest and when it is shortest, and the two days when the day and the night are of equal length. In Ireland, by contrast, two turning points of the year occurred at February 1, about halfway between the winter solstice and the spring equinox, and May 1, halfway between the spring equinox and the summer solstice; the remaining two occurred at August 1 and November 1.

- Each of these dates had a corresponding festival that was connected in some way to the rhythms of the agricultural year. The feast on February 1 was called Imbolc; it was a lambing festival. The May 1 feast was called

Beltaine, and it corresponded to the date when cattle were driven out to the summer pastures.

- On August 1 was the feast of Lughnasa, which was a harvest festival. The feast was named for the god Lugh. November 1 was the date of the festival of Samhain, which celebrated the return of the cattle from the summer pastures and the slaughtering of animals for the winter.

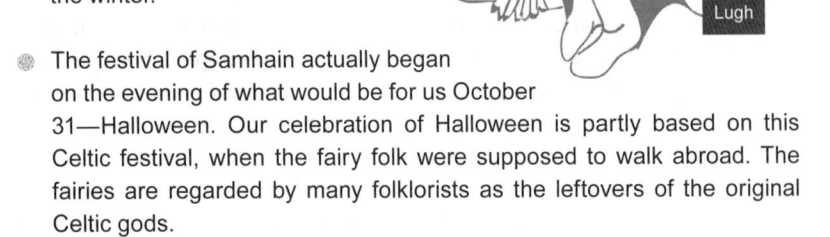

Lugh

- The festival of Samhain actually began on the evening of what would be for us October 31—Halloween. Our celebration of Halloween is partly based on this Celtic festival, when the fairy folk were supposed to walk abroad. The fairies are regarded by many folklorists as the leftovers of the original Celtic gods.

The Celtic Gods

- One of our difficulties in understanding the Celtic gods is the lack of good evidence. The classical authors are not as helpful here as they might be, because they had a habit of just equating any gods they came across among other peoples with gods they recognized in their own pantheon.

- In some cases, we cannot see Celtic religion until Roman rule brought literacy to the Celtic-speaking regions. One good place to find Celtic gods is on Latin inscriptions on votive tablets. These were records of donations or sacrifices offered to the gods, or requests that the god or goddess punish an enemy of the donor. An example is the famous curse tablets at Aquae Sulis (modern-day Bath) that are dedicated to the goddess Sulis

Minerva, a composite deity with both Celtic and Roman traits. There are even two rare curse tablets that seem to have been written in a Celtic language, probably the ancestor of the British language. Depictions of gods also appear on sculptures.

- The god Lugh—associated with lightning, storms, and perhaps war—seems to have been important in many places across the areas discussed in this course. Place names based on the god Lugh can be found widely scattered around Europe. For example, the city of Lyons in France was once called Lugdunum, which comes from a Gaulish name meaning "fortress of the god Lugh."

- Other deities seem to have been worshiped rather widely across the Celtic territories, such as the horse goddess Epona or the fertility goddess Brig. Like Lugh, Brig is spread across the map of Europe, and her name is preserved in the name Britain. But there are dozens and dozens of other Celtic deities who seem to have been worshiped in a far more isolated fashion.

Suggested Reading

Freeman, *Ireland and the Classical World*.
———, *The Philosopher and the Druids*.
———, *War, Women, and Druids*.
Green, *The Celtic World*, part 8.
Piggott, *The Druids*.

Questions to Consider

1. What are the challenges to reconstructing Celtic religion?

2. To what extent did Celtic religious practices depart from classical norms, and to what extent did they converge with them?

Lecture

7

Celtic Britain and Roman Britain

This lecture concentrates on Britain. First, we'll examine the question of whether the inhabitants of Britain can be called Celts, and if so, in what sense. Then, we'll look at what life was like for the people of Britain both before and after Britain was occupied by Rome.

An Important Question

- It used to be easy to answer the question of whether or not Britons were Celts: The old answer was of course they were. The earliest proper names we have from Britain are definitely in a Celtic language. By the time of the first Roman invasion in the 1st century BC, they were producing objects in the La Tène style of art.

- The old model for the Celts would have said that Britain became Celtic through invasion. Celtic warriors from Central Europe brought the total Celtic package with them: language, art, culture, the cult of the severed head, and so on.

- But there are some problems with the evidence. The first and most obvious problem is that no ancient author calls the inhabitants of Britain Celts. They did call people on the continent Celts, but not the people of Britain.

- Another problem comes with the linguistic evidence. We have two major groups of Celtic languages today: Brythonic and Goidelic, corresponding roughly to the languages spoken in Britain and the languages spoken in Ireland. This division within the Celtic language family poses a problem for the invasion model. Modern linguists mostly believe that the Goidelic branch of Celtic developed earlier than the Brythonic branch.

- If that's the case, the timing of a Celtic invasion of the British Isles and Ireland is shaky. Scholars proposed an explanation that relied on two Celtic invasions instead of one. First, an original ground of Goidelic speakers came to Britain and then went to Ireland; second, a new wave of Brythonic

66 | Lecture 7 Celtic Britain and Roman Britain

speakers followed and conquered Britain, but did not go to Ireland. This two-invasion model seems a little too complicated to be plausible.

- Plus, there are problems with the archaeological evidence. There is no evidence for large-scale movements of people. Usually, big population movements bring corresponding lifestyle changes—like housing styles—but this didn't occur in Britain.

- Another objection to the idea of a Celtic invasion comes from a very modern technique: the study of DNA. If the invasion hypothesis is true, then we ought to be able to see a connection in the DNA of modern British people with the DNA of Central Europeans around the areas of Hallstatt and La Tène. But recent studies have shown that the inhabitants of Britain are not closely related to the inhabitants of central Europe, so if the Celts were from the Hallstatt/La Tène region, they did not invade Britain.

A New Theory

- In recent years, scholars have replaced the invasion hypothesis with a different model altogether. They now believe in a process of Celticization by diffusion rather than invasion.

- A scholar named Lisa Bond has come up with a very evocative way to distinguish the two models: she calls the invasion model the diaspora model, and she calls the diffusion model the meme model. The diaspora model is the idea that art styles spread with a people as the people spread out from an original homeland.

- The meme model is completely different. Instead of the people bringing the art style with them, the art style spreads without people moving from place to place, like a meme spreads today on the internet, without any of the people involved migrating at all.

- A possible mechanism for this spread of Celtic culture was trade, particularly the metal trade. Britain was a major center of metals, particularly tin, copper, and iron, especially from Cornwall and Wales.

- The trade in metals probably created a merchant elite all along the Atlantic Coast of Europe. These were Celtic-speaking areas. It may be that Celtic speech and certain aspects of Celtic culture made their way to Britain by this route. The art may have taken a different route, directly from Central Europe (remember, the art never made it to Spain). This would create fusion in Britain of Celtic speech with La Tène art, both of which were probably associated with high status, and then the language spread.

- The question remains: Are we entitled to call the inhabitants of Britain Celts? It's likely that we are, as long as we know what we mean by the term. We are calling them Celts because they spoke a Celtic language, and while there are a lot of scholars who expend a lot of energy trying to stop people from calling the Britons Celts, it's such an ingrained habit by now that it isn't worth worrying about too much.

Britain and the Romans

- Next, the lecture turns to what Britain was like before the Roman conquest and how Britain fared under Roman rule. Britain in the Iron Age was not politically united. Pre-Roman Britain was divided among many tribes. However, this was a fairly prosperous society with elites that became wealthy, especially in the south and east, which had much richer agricultural lands.

- In 55 BC, while Caesar was in the midst of his campaigns in Gaul, he led an expedition to Britain, but it wasn't very successful. He came back the next year with a greater number of soldiers and managed to get some local British tribes to promise submission to Rome. Then, Caesar left. Nothing much more happened between Rome and Britain for about a century.

- In that century, of course, a lot had changed for Rome. The Roman Republic had fallen, largely due to Caesar's own actions, and an emperor now led Rome. The imperial administration had grown much more elaborate. The second time Rome encountered Britain, it was as more of an official enterprise.

- It all started in 43 AD under Emperor Claudius. He decided he wanted a military triumph to boast about, and Britain was one of the last feasible places the Romans could conquer. But unlike Julius Caesar, Claudius was no general. He had his soldiers plan and carry out the campaign, with a much larger number of men than Julius Caesar had had. Claudius showed up at the end to take the credit.

- This time, though, the Romans were planning to stay. They made arrangements to collect tribute from a lot of the British tribes, particularly in the south and east. Over the course of the next 20 years or so, they established legions at several important strongholds in Britain, including Londinium, which of course became London, and Eboracum, which became York. They connected fortified sites throughout the country with roads.

Claudius

- The British tribes responded in various ways to Roman rule. Some of the tribes, particularly the ones in the south and east who had already had a lot of contact with the Roman province of Gaul, were actually quite happy to collaborate with the new Roman regime. In fact, in about 50 AD, the queen of the Brigantes tribe, Cartimandua, actively helped the Romans to suppress the resistance of the Catuvellauni tribe by turning over their leader, Caractacus, to the Roman authorities.

The Celtic World | 69

- Conversely, the Iceni tribe of eastern England broke out into a terrifying rebellion in 60 AD. This rebellion nearly swept the Romans out of Britain. But the Romans prevailed, and they reestablished control in the southern part of the island. The Roman authorities had clearly been spooked, and one of the decisions they made over the next couple of decades was to concentrate their efforts in Britain in the south and east, where they had had the most success thus far.

The Caledonians

- The Romans did mount a major campaign into the north of Britain in 83 AD under the leadership of a general named Agricola. He had a son-in-law named Tacitus who was a good historian. The Romans had been trying for many years to bring the northern British tribe known as the Caledonians to battle, but the Caledonians wisely declined to fight the Romans, who were much better armed and disciplined.

- Instead, the Caledonians would appear and disappear, never quite providing a target that the Romans could strike at. Finally, the Romans brought the Caledonians to battle by marching north into Caledonian territory just as the harvest was being brought in. The Romans went straight for the granaries. The Caledonians had to fight or starve.

- The Romans and Caledonians fought a major battle at a site known as Mons Graupius, somewhere in what is now Scotland, but the location of the battle has never been positively identified. It was apparently a complete rout. Tacitus tells us that 10,000 Caledonian soldiers were killed, while on the Roman side, only 360 auxiliary troops died; the Romans had not even had to deploy their main legionary forces. Rome seemed poised to bring all of the island of Britain under its direct control.

- It was not to be. Agricola was recalled to Rome, given a triumph, and sent to rule another province elsewhere in the empire. Tacitus implies that Rome had conquered all of Britain, only to let it slip from her grasp.

Walls

- Under Emperor Hadrian, in the early 2nd century, the Romans built a wall clear across what is now northern England, from the mouth of the Tyne River in the east to the mouth of the Solway Firth in the west, to mark off the territory they were prepared to defend. To the south of the wall was civilized territory. To the north there were barbarian tribes such as the Picts and Scots, people who painted themselves blue and fought naked. The Romans were just as happy not to mess with them.

- They found out why they shouldn't mess with the Picts by trying to build a wall a little further north a few decades after Hadrian's Wall. This was the Antonine Wall, which ran from the Firth of Forth in the east, near what is now Edinburgh, to the Firth of Clyde in the west, near what is now Glasgow. The Antonine Wall proved to be too far north, and the Romans had to abandon it. Hadrian's Wall became the northern boundary of the Roman Empire.

- In the colonized southern region, the Roman province of Britain fell into two broad zones. First, there was the southern and eastern part of the

Hadrian's Wall

The Celtic World | 71

province. This was the area with the most fertile agricultural land. It was the easiest for the Romans to conquer and eventually looked fairly Roman.

- The other zone, to the north and west, looked quite different. Here the landscape was hilly and rocky, and it was much harder to set up the kinds of settlements the Romans were used to. The local tribes were less cooperative. The Roman military presence in these areas, especially in what is now Wales, Cornwall, and the northwest, had to be much stronger. They were largely successful at preventing serious revolts, but there was certainly no chance that they would be able to hold the province if the soldiers weren't there.

Impact on Celtic Speakers

- For the native, British Celtic speakers under Roman rule, some things stayed the same and other things changed. In the cities, the language of daily life was Latin. The main cultural trends in the life of the Roman Empire eventually made their way to Britain (trends such as artistic styles, styles of dress, and religion). From about the 3rd century, Christianity appeared in Britain and got a secure foothold in the towns. Of course, it had plenty of competition. There were dozens of other cults being practiced in the British towns, just like in all the other Roman cities.

- In the countryside, the Latin language probably did not penetrate very far. These rural inhabitants probably spoke little if any Latin; their language was British. Few of these country dwellers would have adopted Christianity; many would have continued to follow their pagan gods throughout the period of Roman occupation. Their field patterns stayed the same throughout the Roman period and beyond.

- However, these British inhabitants were Romanized in a very important sense: They used a lot of Roman goods. Examples include pottery that had been mass-produced, glassware, and iron nails for building.

- The diet of these Celtic-speaking inhabitants also changed as a result of the Roman presence in Britain. They began growing and eating fruits originally brought in from Italy, such as apples. One other way we can see the penetration of Roman culture into everyday life in Britain is the presence of Roman coins in small denominations, even on quite rural sites. The economy was becoming more monetized; even very low-level exchanges were now taking place by means of money rather than barter.

- But there was something behind this increase in monetary circulation other than pure market forces: taxation. The Roman state needed huge amounts of money to pay for its military infrastructure, a large portion of which was spent on Britain. These taxes were collected throughout the empire and in many cases spent locally to pay the Roman military garrisons and provide them with food and other supplies. Ironically, the Roman occupation was a huge stimulus to the British economy.

Suggested Reading

Aldhouse-Green, *Boudica Britannia*.

Ellis, *The Celtic Empire*, chapters 10, 11, and 14.

James, *The World of the Celts*, chapter 5.

Koch and Carey, *The Celtic Heroic Age*.

Litton, *The Celts: An Illustrated History*, chapter 2.

Questions to Consider

1. How has the picture of how Britain came to be Celtic changed over time?

2. How did the various regions of the island of Britain experience Roman rule differently?

Lecture

8

Celts and the Picts in Scotland

The previous lecture looked at Britain both before and after Roman occupation, concentrating mostly on the areas that the Romans conquered, primarily in the south and east. This lecture shifts to focus on what was going on in northern Britain, the area that never fully came under Roman control. Of particular focus are the Picts, a group that shared northern Britain with many other peoples.

The Picts

- At the time of the Roman invasion, various tribes inhabited Scotland, including the people later known as Picts, who probably spoke a form of Brythonic Celtic related to Welsh. Only over the course of subsequent centuries did the Picts diverge from the other tribes of northern Britain and forge a distinctive identity.

- They were not called the Picts until the late 3rd century, when a crisis in the Roman Empire led several Roman authors to start calling attention to various groups of people on the Roman frontiers, including the area north of Hadrian's Wall. These authors wrote panegyrics, or praise poems, about various Roman emperors and their accomplishments. One of these texts gives the first mention of the term Picts, whom it describes as half-naked savages. This was a period when the Romans faced quite a few enemies.

- There was also a second way in which the Romans "invented" the Picts, and this goes beyond terminology. The group of tribes north of Hadrian's Wall that came to be known as the Picts were similar to the Britons who lived south of Hadrian's Wall. However, they were not Romanized.

- By the late 3rd century, when the term Picti (which means "painted ones") appeared, the two areas of Britain had diverged. The Britons south of the wall had adopted Roman customs (and presumably were wearing more clothes and fewer tattoos); the peoples north of the wall had not.

Woad plant

- A widespread idea is that the Picts painted themselves blue. Julius Caesar tells us that the Celts supposedly got blue pigment from the woad plant and that they used it to decorate their bodies. But there are no specific accounts of woad being used in Scotland to paint human skin. We don't know if the Picts actually painted themselves blue.

Rome Versus the Picts

- The Picts were a military threat to Roman Britain. In 367 to 368 AD and at a few other times, they seem to have allied with groups of people coming from Ireland, who may have constituted the later Irish kingdom of Dál Riata that straddled the sea between northeastern Ireland and southwestern Scotland.

- This so-called barbarian conspiracy started off a war that lasted on and off well into the 5th century, and at one point, the Picts and their allies had established temporary control of the Roman province of Britain. This was a sophisticated strategic effort that required extensive knowledge of Roman defenses.

- However, Roman Britain survived as a Christianized province well into the 5th century. It was probably from somewhere in the northern part of the province of Britain that St. Patrick was captured as a slave and taken to northern Ireland.

- St. Patrick had an important confrontation with people who may have come under the general heading of Picts, or at least of northern, un-Romanized Britons. St. Patrick served as a slave in the north of Ireland for six years, during which time he underwent a religious conversion. He had been raised as a Christian, but a fairly lukewarm one. However, the experience of captivity gave him time to pray and reflect, and he felt the call to evangelize the Irish.

St. Patrick

- After his escape, he studied for the priesthood and returned to Ireland to preach the Gospel. It was at some point during his mission that he came up against Coroticus, a British (or Pictish) warlord from southwestern Scotland, who had carried out a massive slave raid in northern Ireland. Many of the victims of this slave raid were newly baptized converts. Coroticus had stolen away the fruits of St. Patrick's missionary labors.

- St. Patrick wrote a letter to Coroticus demanding that these captives be released. In the letter, St. Patrick very ostentatiously refused to call Coroticus a fellow Roman; St. Patrick seemed to think this was a very effective put-down. The Roman label carried with it an assumption that the person so labeled was also a Christian, and Coroticus was at least nominally a Christian.

- The northern Britons had been evangelized starting in the late 4th century, which is what made the participation of Coroticus in the slave trade so heinous in St. Patrick's eyes. The letter was intended to shame Coroticus publicly. Unfortunately, we have no indication that the captives of Coroticus were ever released.

Tribal Confederations

- The picture we get from the St. Patrick incident of political chaos in northern Britain and northern Ireland is probably pretty accurate. There was no unified Pictish kingdom. Instead, there were a number of tribal confederations, much as was the case in Britain when the Romans first arrived.

- These tribal confederations fall into two rough categories. Some of them belong in the Pictish category, but historians classify other tribal groupings as British, such as the kingdom of Goutodin.

- As for the difference between the British and Pictish classifications: Part of the difference could be language. But there may have been other cultural and political forces at work that slowly drove the inhabitants of northern Britain to line up in two distinct ethnic groupings, despite the fact that they were originally very similar to each other.

- The origins of this division are obscure, but by the period of the Roman withdrawal from Britain, in the northern part of the island, there were two main power blocs. In the territory that would later be Scotland were some peoples who were Pictish and other peoples who were British, but even within these two main categories, there was no political unity.

- To add to this complicated picture, there were newcomers to northern Britain coming in from two directions. Starting largely in the 5th century, Irish settlers arrived in the north and west, particularly in the islands off the west coast of Scotland; in fact, these Irish settlers were known as the Scotti, and, much later they would give their name to the people of Scotland. It's confusing that Scotland is named after an Irish tribe, but this course will call them Irish from now on.

- Around 500 or so, groups of Germanic-speaking peoples called Angles began colonizing northern Britain; the Angles gave us the first element in the term *Anglo-Saxon*. They started pushing fairly far north into what is now Scotland, and they spoke a language that is related to our modern English language. Their advance into the Scottish Lowlands in this period is the main reason the Scots speak English today. There is a distinct dialect (or language) called Scots, but it is extremely closely related to English.

Questions

- There are many unresolved questions about the Picts. We are not sure, for instance, whether the Picts lived only in Scotland or whether there were Picts in northern Ireland as well. There are hints that there may have been Picts in Ireland because there are signs that there was a group of people in Ireland, especially in the north, who were regarded by the Irish as ethnically distinct from them. These people were called the Cruithin.

- Northern Britain was very strongly connected to the rest of the island of Britain. It was not cut off by Hadrian's Wall, either before or after the Romans withdrew their legions. Just as the very famous figure of St. Patrick can exemplify the ties between northern Britain and Ireland, so another famous figure can tell us something about how northern Britain is tied to southern Britain: namely, King Arthur.

- There is a very early poem in Welsh called "The Gododdin" that takes place in what is now Scotland, and it's probably most famous today because it contains the first mention of a warrior named Arthur. It takes place around 600. The poem depicts a raid by the men of the British kingdom of Gododdin on the Anglian fortress of Catraeth, which ended in a disastrous defeat for the Britons.

- Back to the Picts: If the story of the British in the north is largely one of retrenchment and defeat, as the areas of British speech were slowly squeezed out, then the story of the Picts is very different. With the Picts, we see political consolidation, at least for a few brief but glorious centuries.

- An important element in the study of the Picts is their language. We don't know as much as we would like to about the Pictish language, because we have only a few inscriptions to go on. These tend to be concentrated in the north and east of what is now Scotland.

- There have been various theories about the origins of Pictish. All of these theories have to be based on a very small number of words, largely personal names, which is not at all ideal for trying to reconstruct a language. One theory suggested that Pictish was related to Irish, while another suggested it might even be related to English. These theories have been discounted by modern linguists; they just don't hold up to linguistic scrutiny.

- The strangest theory, but potentially the most intriguing one, is that Pictish might be a pre-Indo-European language that had somehow survived the supposed arrival of the Celts in northern Britain. This theory has the merit of making the Picts seem like a special remnant of a very deep prehistoric past. But it's just not true.

- Linguists and historians have now largely agreed that Pictish is a Celtic language closely related to Gaulish, though they are not exactly sure how distinct it was from British. They also cannot be sure whether it became distinct from British while both languages were evolving on the island of

Britain, or if the two languages, Pictish and British, made their way to Britain independently.

- Some Pictish inscriptions use the Latin alphabet. But other inscriptions use a totally different system of writing called *ogam*. This system probably came from Ireland, where it was fairly widespread from the 4th to the 6th centuries, but it was also present in various parts of western Britain and in Scotland.

Picture Stones

- There is one more mystery about the Picts that we really don't have a solution to. That is the meaning of the Pictish picture stones. These stones feature repeating motifs that are common to the whole area of Pictish inscriptions, so they seem to belong to some kind of standardized pictorial vocabulary or formulary, but nobody knows what they represent.

- Modern scholars have given these symbols names, such as the double disc and the z-rod, but they don't really know what they represent. The strangest one is the so-called Pictish beast. It doesn't seem to represent any known animal. It looks a little like a seahorse or possibly a dolphin, but it's hard to tell.

Conclusion

- The Picts are less mysterious than we used to think. They grew out of the same political and cultural developments as occurred in the rest of Britain. They are not some strange remnant of a pre-Celtic past. They were as much Celts as anybody else in Britain, which is to say, they were definitely speaking a Celtic language, though nobody called them Celts at the time.

- The Picts were a success story. They seem to have banded together and created a fairly stable, unified kingdom, which was always quite an achievement in this period. Starting in the period around the fall of Rome, several Pictish kingdoms emerged, primarily in northern and eastern Scotland.

- A 10th-century document called the "Pictish Chronicle" says that there were seven of these kingdoms, each ruled by one of the seven sons of a single king. This is suspiciously tidy, but it does express the reality that the Picts were slowly cohering. By the 7th century, the most powerful Pictish kingdom, the kingdom of Fortriu in northeastern Scotland, probably exercised a form of hegemony over the smaller Pictish territories.

- But the Picts were also very open to outside influences. They apparently patronized Irish-speaking bards, which foreshadowed the ultimate replacement of Pictish language and culture by Irish in the years to come.

- The takeaway from this exploration of northern Britain is that the later kingdom of Scotland is probably the most diverse in origin of any of the so-called Celtic regions. It developed out of a mixture of British, Pictish, Irish, and English elements. Scotland became even more multi-ethnic in the Viking period, when people from Scandinavia entered the mix.

Suggested Reading

Hudson, *The Picts*.

Jackson, *The Gododdin*.

Laing and Laing, *Celtic Britain and Ireland*, chapter 6.

Skinner, trans., *The Confession of Saint Patrick and Letter to Coroticus*.

Thomas, *Celtic Britain*, chapter 5.

Questions to Consider

1. How are the Picts related to the Celts?

2. What remains mysterious about the Picts?

Lecture

9

Prehistoric Ireland and the Celts

This lecture focuses on Ireland, and Ireland will play a very important role in the course from this point on. There is a lot to say about the early history of Ireland, but this lecture focuses on a single question: How did Ireland wind up as the Celtic-speaking country it clearly was by the time it enters the historical record? The lecture looks at this question in three ways that correspond to three different moments in time. First, it looks at what the early Irish thought they knew about their own prehistoric past and their national traditions. Second, it examines what scholars have made of those traditions. Finally, the lecture turns to recent changes in how scholars understand Irish history.

Keep in mind two things about Ireland during this lecture: One, it was never conquered by the Romans, and two, because Ireland was not conquered by Rome, Irish society was not literate until the conversion to Christianity. The conversion started in the late 4th century but didn't take hold enough to produce many written texts until several centuries later. Therefore, it's one thing to say that the Irish kept their traditions while the rest of the Celtic world was succumbing to Roman domination. It's another thing entirely to know exactly what those traditions were.

Pre-Christian Ireland

- To learn about pre-Christian Ireland, we have to rely mostly on texts written down after the conversion to Christianity. Fortunately, there are a lot of these texts. Ireland can boast not just the largest body of vernacular texts in a Celtic language, but in fact the largest body of texts to survive in any vernacular language from early medieval Europe.

- These texts come in all varieties, from legal material to genealogical material. There is also an extensive body of texts that we would broadly consider literary, though they have elements of history and mythology mixed in. The key text for this lecture, *The Book of Invasions*, falls in that category. So we actually have quite a few texts that can give us a picture of the pre-Christian past.

- The main origin legend of the Irish is found in *The Book of Invasions*. (In Irish, the text's name is *Lebor Gabála Érenn*.) According to this text, Ireland was populated by a series of invasions by a series of different invaders, totalling six waves of invasion in all. The text began to take shape starting in the 8th century, but we have it in versions that really crystallized in the 11th and 12th centuries. It's a difficult-to-read text that includes elements like floods, giants, magical mist, and battles.

- The story is quite complicated, but here's how it ends: After wandering for 300 years, a group called the Gaels landed in Spain and conquered it. Their leader, a man named Mil, ruled over Spain. They built a tall tower. After Mil died, his sons Emer and Eremon ruled in his place.

- One day, their uncle Ith went to the top of the tower and thought he could see the shadow of a land far away. He told his nephews Emer and Eremon that he would like to visit that land, so he set off with some companions. When he got to that land, which turned out to be Ireland, he found the ruling Túatha de Danann in the midst of an internal quarrel over property.

- Seeing that Ith was a wise man, the contending parties asked Ith for his judgment on the case. He essentially told them that this was a beautiful, rich country, and there was enough here for everyone. Instead of making them feel better, this got them thinking that Ith was planning to invade and settle there, so they killed him.

- When the survivors of the expedition got back to Spain, Ith's nephews were outraged and decided to avenge their uncle, so they set off for Ireland. The Túatha were tricky customers, so they enveloped Ireland in a shroud; the sons of Mil ended up sailing around Ireland three times before finally landing. They demanded one of three things: battle or kingship or judgment.

- In the negotiations, the Túatha agreed that the sons of Mil would rule Ireland henceforth if they could first sail over nine waves and then return. The Gaels got in their ships and sailed away to meet the challenge, but it was of course a trick. The crafty Túatha called up a supernatural wind that sent up huge waves. Luckily, Emer and Eremon had another brother named Amergin, who was a bard. He sang a song to the island of Ireland, asking that they be allowed to land, and the winds quieted.

- When the sons of Mil got to Ireland, they defeated the Túatha in battle, and they fled over the sea. (Some versions of the story say they were exiled below the ground; this is the origin of fairy mounds.) The sons of Mil then divided Ireland into two halves.

- Eremon the elder got the northern half, and Emer got the south. They were the ancestors of the two major ruling dynasties of Ireland. Everyone in Ireland is thus a descendant either of the sons of Mil or of the people they conquered. This story is what the Irish believed about how their island was peopled down through the Middle Ages and beyond.

Sons of Mil

Skepticism

- Starting as early as the 16th century, scholars in other countries, especially England, began to cast some doubt upon this story. Skeptical English scholars started to raise concerns about the giants, magic mists, and so forth. It gradually dawned on most people, even the Irish themselves, that the stories in *The Book of Invasions* could not be literally true in every detail.

- This brings up the debate about the way in which we can use Irish sources written down after the Irish converted to Christianity. The older view of this question is that people could actually trust these sources very much. There is a very famous formulation by the great historian and linguist Kenneth Hurlstone Jackson, who wrote an article in 1964 that claimed that early Irish texts could be read as if they opened up a "window on the Iron Age."

- Scholars like Jackson became known as the nativist school because they believed that what one sees in early Irish texts is a fairly pure representation of authentic Irish tradition. They argued that Irish literature was essentially conservative, and that it had preserved an unbroken link to the remote pagan past.

- The nativist argument rested on two main theories. The first theory is that there did indeed exist, at one time, a common Indo-European culture that spread all over Europe with the spread of Indo-European languages, of which Celtic is a major subgroup. Then a common Celtic culture spread, of which the Irish language is a major constituent. The second theory is that such a culture could genuinely be preserved over very long periods by oral transmission.

- But the nativists needed a way to explain how such texts could really preserve material from thousands of years ago. The breakthrough came in the late 1950s and early 1960s from work done by Albert Lord and Denys Page on the way oral traditions are preserved.

- Lord and Page argued from their studies of the *Iliad* and other Greek texts that oral tradition could preserve a record of archaic society and remain unchanged when it was finally written down. They thought that the *Iliad* probably did represent a work first composed in the remote past and handed down orally for many centuries until it was finally committed to writing.

- But even if one accepts that the texts do represent the survival of an ancient tradition, there is another big question remaining: Why would Christian scholars in the period after the conversion take the trouble to preserve all this pagan material? The nativists argued that the early Irish scholars, Christians though they were, had a deep respect for and love of their heritage, and that they wanted to preserve it before it was lost. The nativists imagined the early scholars as heritage buffs who were not especially troubled by the pagan material they were recording; it was their native history, after all.

- The nativists do reluctantly concede that the texts do show a few signs of monastic censorship (characters who are obviously gods or goddesses are sometimes depicted as mere human beings—like the Túatha de Danann). But they're willing to overlook these few lapses and cling gratefully to the mass of the authentic material that the texts preserve.

Ideas on Origins

- Many 19th-century scholars conceived of the Celts as originating in Central Europe and spreading outward by conquest. They supposedly arrived in Britain and Ireland as invaders, in either one wave or two waves, depending on the theory. This sounds an awful lot like *The Book of Invasions*.

- Of course, the Celtic origin theory has the Celts arriving from Central Europe, not Spain, but perhaps there is even an explanation for the otherwise very odd-seeming Spanish connection. There is a region in northwest Spain known as Galicia that has Celtic roots—the name is etymologically related to the word *Gaelic*. Perhaps, many scholars have argued, the story of the sons of Mil represents the memory of real a migration from Spain by people of Gaelic speech.

- Scholars up through the mid-20th century were trying to figure out ways to harmonize *The Book of Invasions* with their ideas of how the Celts spread out from Hallstatt and La Tène, or possibly even from Galicia. The nativist view is thus a very optimistic view of how we can use these Irish texts in combination with modern scholarship to paint a picture of how Ireland came to be a Celtic nation.

- However, since the 1990s, the pendulum has swung in a more pessimistic direction with regard to how much we can use these texts to tell us what pre-Christian Irish traditions actually were. More recent scholars such as Kim McCone have done a lot of textual analysis.

- They are much more skeptical than earlier scholars like Kenneth Jackson about the notion that these texts purely preserve the pre-Christian past. For one thing, they have found more Christian material in these texts than the earlier scholars did. The narratives have often been shaped to conform to Biblical models. For example, the narrative of *The Book of Invasions* has been harmonized with the chronology of the Bible.

- Furthermore, the Bible is not the only non-Irish text that has influenced *The Book of Invasions*. *The Book of Invasions* contains mermaids, and people needed to put wax in their ears to resist the mermaids' siren call. That is straight out of the *Odyssey*. These texts represent a fascinating mishmash of native traditions and Christian and classical influences; the task of disentangling these elements to recover a pure lost original is probably hopeless.

- Furthermore, new doubt has been cast on the idea of oral transmission as an inherently conservative process. New work on living oral traditions in Africa has shown that they are more dynamic than people used to think. Modern concerns end up creeping into ancient stories. Perhaps we can't be sure the Irish stories go back unchanged to the Iron Age, let alone the remote Indo-European past.

- The most recent scholarship seriously doubts whether we can make any actual correlations between the stories and the prehistoric past, and they say further that the medieval Irish people who wrote the legends down weren't trying to do that either. They were trying to create a blend of old traditions and new traditions.

- Furthermore, we have the two kinds of non-written evidence: archaeological evidence and DNA analysis. Neither kind of evidence supports the idea of Ireland being peopled by a series of invasions. Archaeological evidence does not show signs of a large-scale movement of peoples into Ireland at the time of the supposed Celtic migrations in the 3rd century or so BC.

- But it's very interesting to see that while DNA evidence does not show strong correlations between the inhabitants of Ireland and the inhabitants of Central Europe, it does show links between the Irish and the inhabitants of the whole European Atlantic seaboard, including Spain. That opens the intriguing possibility that the authors of *The Book of Invasions* may have (accidentally) been right.

Suggested Reading

Carey, *A New Introduction to Lebor Gabála Érenn*.

Cross and Slover, *Ancient Irish Tales*, pp. 3–27.

Jackson, *The Oldest Irish Tradition*.

McCone, *Pagan Past and Christian Present in Early Irish Literature*.

Questions to Consider

1. How have ideas about the origin myth of the Irish people changed over time?
2. How much can we see the Irish Iron Age through early Irish texts?

Lecture 10

Celtic Britain after Rome

This lecture returns to a topic from a previous lecture and focuses on what happened to the Celtic-speaking regions of Britain after the withdrawal of the Roman legions. It used to be thought that Roman Britain was destroyed by Germanic invaders, the famous Angles, Saxons, and Jutes. Supposedly, these invaders exterminated the local Romanized but Celtic-speaking population.

According to the traditional narrative, Celtic-speaking Britons were progressively pushed westward by the advance of the newcomers. The result was that the island of Britain was divided into an English-speaking England in the south and east, with a fringe of Celtic speakers in the southwest, west, and northwest. But it turns out that the story is more complicated. The retreat of Celtic speech and culture may have actually been due much more to assimilation than to invasion.

The End Begins

- The height of Roman rule in Britain was the 2nd century, featuring prosperous villas and cities. However, starting in the 3rd century, Britain began to be attacked by barbarians. This was a crisis that affected not just Britain but the whole of the Roman Empire.

- Britain got hit from two directions. From the west, there were raiders from Ireland. These people were known as the Scotti because some of them would later settle in Scotland and give their name to the country. There were also raiders from the northwest coast of Europe. They were from Germanic-speaking tribes in what are now the Low Countries and northern Germany.

- The Romans counteracted this threat by appointing a commander to defend the southeast coast. He was known as the Count of the Saxon Shore. In 367 AD, Britain was hit by a perfect storm of barbarian raiders.

This episode is known as the barbarian conspiracy; that's what it was called by a contemporary Roman writer named Ammianus Marcellinus.

- The Irish to the west and the Picts to the north got together to attack Britain; at the same time, Germanic raiders were hitting the coast of Gaul, so the Roman authorities there couldn't help. The Count of the Saxon Shore was killed. All seemed lost until a large Roman army showed up, under the future Roman emperor Theodosius, to save the day. The same scenario was repeated a few years later, and the Roman general Stilicho had to come and help. But that kind of rescue was never going to be available to Roman Britain again.

- Things were steadily getting worse for Rome, and it was heading toward its fall. In 406 AD, there was an unusually cold winter, and the Rhine River froze. Large numbers of barbarians from northern Europe simply walked across the river into Roman territory and raided all over the Roman province of Gaul.

- This was a threat to the security of Rome itself, so Emperor Honorius decided on a fateful step. He ordered the Roman legions in Britain to withdraw to the continent, and he told the residents of Britain, essentially, they were on their own.

- The traditional picture of the 5th century is one of barbarian invasions. Without the Roman troops there to defend the province, the way was clear for large-scale raiding. We have a rather poignant record of the reaction of the local population to this alarming turn of events.

- This is preserved in a work by an author from the 6th century named Gildas. He recorded a very plaintive request for help that the authorities in Britain sent to a Roman commander in Gaul in the middle of the 5th century. The letter reads: "The barbarians push us back to the sea, the sea pushes us back to the barbarians; between these two kinds of death, we are either drowned or slaughtered." Gildas noted that Britain got no help in return.

The Problem Changes

- The story of invasion is very much the tale that later written sources tell us, but there is a problem. The archaeological remains from the 5th century don't show much evidence of warfare. Instead, there was a rather peaceful infiltration. That is because, in the 5th century, the nature of the barbarian problem changed.

- Up until then, mostly the barbarians had been raiding. They would come, grab what they wanted, perhaps burn the rest, kill some people, and then leave. Starting in the mid-5th century, they started staying. Permanent settlements appeared in Britain, especially in the south and east.

- These people probably brought women and children with them, but there is also evidence in the DNA of contemporary British cemeteries that there was considerable intermarriage with the native population. The process of assimilation seems to have taken place over several generations.

- Some of the British inhabitants, especially the elites, moved west, north, and southwest into the Celtic Fringe. As far as we can tell, though, many of the British just blended in with the new culture the settlers brought with them. Over time, they adopted the speech of the newcomers. This is why there is almost no trace left of the British language in modern English. The British simply stopped speaking British and started speaking the language that ultimately became English.

- But this assimilation, important as it was, was only part of the story. In the late 5th and early 6th centuries, there may have been a concerted effort to push back against the new settlers. The British writer Gildas says that at the end of the 5th century, a great war leader emerged who fought 12 great battles against the barbarians. The last of these battles, at Mount Badon, was a great victory that halted the advance of the barbarians for 50 years (that is, right up to the time when Gildas was writing, when things were getting bad again).

King Arthur

- This statement by Gildas seems to be the earliest evidence we have for the existence of the figure who later became known as King Arthur. It's not much to go on. Gildas calls this person a war leader, not a king. He doesn't give him the name Arthur or any other name. Still, there is some evidence in the archaeological record that there was indeed a 50-year halt in the advance of Germanic settlement in Britain.

- We don't know if Arthur really existed, or if he did, if he was actually called Arthur. But there are two main things we need to take away from this question of whether or not Arthur was real. The first is that the story of the leader Gildas describes does capture a real phenomenon. The British were retreating, at least in terms of their language, culture, and political authority, and the Germanic settlers were advancing, whether this was due to assimilation or to military defeat.

- The second important point is this was a step toward a legend. The story of Arthur had quite a future, and he would later become a Celtic hero who was also adopted by the English.

Consequences

- The progressive Anglicization of eastern Britain led to the areas of Celtic speech becoming more and more isolated from each other. Two areas where British speech survived for a time were a region called the Old North and Cornwall. The only area where a Celtic language has survived continuously to the present is Wales.

- Wales managed to keep its culture and its language. At the other end of the spectrum is the Old North, where Celtic speech died out in the Middle Ages, in some cases as early as the 7th or 8th century. Finally, Cornwall is at something like a halfway point on the spectrum between the Old North and Wales.

- It lost its political independence earlier than the Old North, but it managed to keep its language far longer, down to the 18th century. Modern efforts to revive Cornish today have been at least somewhat successful.

- There are even fledgling efforts to revive the Cumbric language in what is now northern England, but they might have less success than the rather modest gains that have been made in Cornwall. It has been a thousand years since British speech was used in northern England; it's probably too long ago for a successful revival, but perhaps not.

Suggested Reading

Ellis, *The Cornish Language and Its Literature*.
Fleming, *Britain after Rome*, chapters 1–5.
Koch and Carey, *The Celtic Heroic Age*, pp. 289–317 and 356–368.
Thomas, *Celtic Britain*, chapters 2–4.

Questions to Consider

1. How did the Celtic-speaking inhabitants of Britain respond to Anglo-Saxon settlement?

2. What can literature tell us about connections between the various regions where Celtic speech survived in Britain?

Lecture 11

Brittany and Galicia: Fringe of the Fringe

This lecture discusses not just the Celtic Fringe, but the fringe of the fringe. These are the so-called marginal areas within the Celtic world: Brittany in France and Galicia in Spain. The lecture looks at them through two lenses of marginality.

Two Types of Marginality

- One kind of marginality has to do with where the Celtic areas found themselves with respect to the major powers that came to dominate them. This form of marginality has its roots in the classical period, when the advance of Latin originally marginalized Celtic speakers.

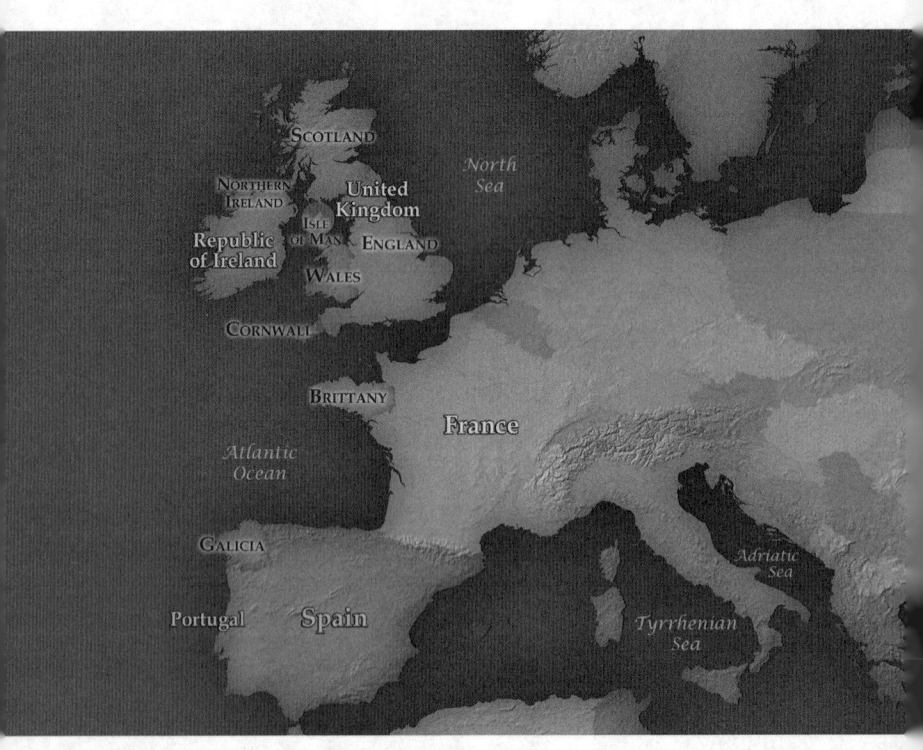

- The other type of marginality has to do with where the different Celtic areas found themselves with respect to the Celtic world as a whole. This second kind of marginality developed much later due to a shift in perspective that came about in the 19th century, when an interest in Celtic heritage arose in Ireland, Wales, and somewhat in Scotland.

- These are the areas where the idea of the Celtic Fringe was embraced wholeheartedly and proudly, but the result ironically was to create a Celtic core centered on western Britain and Ireland. These are areas where the dominant speech that was imposed on the Celtic areas was English. These Celtic areas all had something in common: Their Celtic speech had been replaced by the same foreign language, English, and they were now ruled by the same foreign power, England (as the dominant part of the United Kingdom).

- Brittany in France and Galicia in Spain were now doubly marginal. They were marginal in the nation-states they found themselves within (France and Spain), but they were also marginal within the Celtic world. They did not speak the same mainstream language as the other Celtic enthusiasts, and in some cases, they had to work hard to get into the club of modern Celtic nations.

Background on Brittany

- In the Roman period, Brittany was referred to as Armorica (which means "by the sea" in Gaulish, which was the Celtic language spoken there at the time of Caesar). The peninsula in western France on which Brittany is found is called the Armorican peninsula. Brittany has been a Celtic-speaking region since as far back as our records stretch.

- Brittany has a very long history that stretches thousands of years into the prehistoric period, probably long before the Celtic languages developed. Brittany is one of the areas on the Atlantic coast of Europe that has the largest number of megaliths, large stone monuments that started appearing around 3000 BC.

● The megaliths have nothing specifically to do with the Celts, having been erected long before the cultures we associate with the Celts came into existence. The ancestors of the later Celtic-speaking inhabitants of Brittany may have built them.

● The megaliths probably indicate that the societies along the Atlantic seaboard were quite prosperous, probably due to extensive seaborne trade. But this prosperity seems to have ebbed in Brittany in the middle of the first millennium BC. The economy seems to have picked up, however, in the centuries right before the Roman conquest, when population increased. We can tell this because more land was being brought into cultivation.

104 | Lecture 11 ● Brittany and Galicia: Fringe of the Fringe

- Brittany was changing politically at the same time. In the 2nd century BC, coins began being minted by the three most prominent tribes in the region: the Veneti, the Riedones, and the Namnetes. Other tribes followed suit. By the 1st century BC, trading contacts and political alliances had emerged between the Armorican peninsula and the tribes of northern Gaul on the one hand and southwestern Britain on the other.

- In Caesar's day, various Gaulish tribes inhabited Brittany. We see within the Armorican tribes the same faction fights about policy toward Rome that we see elsewhere in Gaul: Some people thought Roman trade was going to be good for Armorica, while others feared domination by Caesar. It turns out that both parties were right. Caesar thoroughly conquered Gaul in the 50s BC, and Armorica was very much in the thick of the fighting.

- Later, Armorican soldiers were sent to help the Gaulish chieftain Vercingetorix in his last stand against Caesar, but once Vercingetorix was defeated, Armorica settled down to more than four centuries of fairly prosperous Roman rule. This meant a massive infrastructure investment by the Romans. A comprehensive road network was built out. New fortresses and urban settlements were also built.

- All that changed beginning in the 5th century AD, as Roman power throughout northwestern Europe started to decline. At this time, people in southwestern Britain began to migrate to Brittany in substantial numbers from what are now Cornwall and Devon and the adjoining areas.

- The people who came to Brittany from southwestern Britain established dominance

Vercingetorix

The Celtic World | 105

over the Armorican peninsula and slowly expanded eastward. The British speech of the newcomers drove out the speech of the natives, presumably due to the fact that the newcomers were wealthy and powerful, lending them cultural prestige.

- Breton hegemony was established in the Armorican peninsula, and the name of the peninsula was changed to Brittany as a result. The Bretons continued to push east into France, but the Breton advance was finally stopped in the early 10th century by the arrival of new people coming from the east: the Normans, who were themselves newcomers from Scandinavia. Thereafter, the Bretons and the Normans fought border wars, but under the reign of Duke William of Normandy, Brittany finally came under Norman hegemony. The Bretons still had their own duke, but he often fought beside William, very much under William's tutelage.

- William was famous for something beyond bringing Brittany under Norman influence. The Norman Conquest of England in 1066 was hugely important to the history of Brittany, because it effectively reestablished political ties between the island of Britain and Brittany.

- William recruited many Breton soldiers to fight in his army, and there were hundreds of Bretons fighting alongside him at his victorious Battle of Hastings. Many Bretons settled in Britain after Hastings, and some of them gravitated toward Wales, where the language and culture of the people was not far removed from their own.

- This semi-homecoming had important consequences for the culture of all of medieval Europe because this was how King Arthur went mainstream. In the 1130s, a man of mixed Breton and Welsh heritage named Geoffrey of Monmouth set up shop as a cleric in Oxford. There, he produced a text in Latin called the *History of the Kings of Britain* that he claimed to be a translation from an old book written in the British language (which presumably means Welsh in this context).

- The book told the history of Britain from the earliest days down through the reign of King Arthur. However, it's likely Geoffrey of Monmouth made up the detail about the book being translated from an old book. Nevertheless, many people believed him, and the stories in Geoffrey of Monmouth's work became the basis for the smash literary sensation of the 12th century and beyond: Arthurian literature.

Power Struggles

- While Brittany may have been on the geographic margins of France, it played an important part in the power struggles that plagued western France in the 12th century. During this period, the kings of England were also great feudal magnates in France.

- The English kings controlled most of the western seaboard of France, but they were perpetually at war with their supposed feudal overlords, the kings of France. The idea that Arthur had been the leader of a proud people with a glorious past was very popular in Brittany, where the Bretons were chafing under the rule first of the Norman dukes and then of the English kings.

- In the late 12th century, the duke of Brittany had no sons, so the heir to the duchy was his daughter Constance. She was married to Geoffrey Plantagenet, the son of King Henry II of England. The idea was that Geoffrey would eventually rule Brittany as Constance's husband.

- However, Geoffrey died young, before he could take the ducal throne. He left a daughter, Eleanor. But his wife Constance, the heiress to the duchy of Brittany, was pregnant when her husband died. The baby turned out to be a boy. They named him Arthur. By giving the young prince the name of a famous British ruler, the Bretons were making a statement. They were great in the past and they would be great again.

- Unfortunately, Arthur suffered a melancholy fate involving the crusader and English king Richard the Lionheart. Richard was famous for going on crusade, and he was fairly successful in achieving some carefully circumscribed goals in the east, but he didn't manage to capture Jerusalem.

- On his return to Europe, the vassal of one of his most powerful enemies captured him, and England had to pay a huge ransom for him to be released. The rest of his reign was spent cleaning up the damage that was done to his authority in all his domains, both English and French, by his long absence, first on crusade, and then in captivity.

- It was in one such cleanup exercise in 1199 that Richard received a fatal arrow wound. He left several possible heirs. One was his only surviving legitimate brother, Prince John, who was widely loathed. The other possible heir was John's nephew, the 12-year-old Prince Arthur, who was the son of John's deceased older brother, Geoffrey.

- King Philip of France decided to exploit this succession struggle and backed Prince Arthur. It was better for France to have a young and inexperienced king of England instead of a full-grown man, even one as unpopular as John.

- Over the next couple of years, John and Arthur fought for the succession. In 1202, John captured Arthur, and the boy was never seen again. John almost certainly had him killed, though there were some reports that John had done the evil deed himself. John's probable murder of Arthur, among other factors, helped turn public opinion against him, and within a few years, he had lost most of his lands in France to the French king. Brittany reestablished its autonomy within France. It was essentially independent.

- The Bretons clung fiercely to their independence, even in the face of the machinations of two very powerful potential overlords: England and France. They managed to hold off political subordination all the way until the late 15th century, when the ducal line failed in the male line. Anne, duchess of Brittany, married two French kings in succession. This union finally cemented the incorporation of Brittany within the French kingdom.

- Although Breton political autonomy was officially at an end, the Breton language survived, and until fairly recently, it was the most widely spoken of the Celtic languages (even in the 1980s, there were possibly a million speakers of Breton). That number has since declined precipitously, to about half a million speakers. Breton is now outstripped by Welsh in the number of active speakers of each language. Still, the survival of the language is a powerful testament to the strength of Breton identity.

Galicia

- The story of Galicia is in some respects similar to the story of Brittany, but there are also key differences between the two cases. One very important point to start with is that Galicia has had one of the most varied experiences of any of the Celtic-speaking regions.

- Galicia has an unimpeachable Celtic pedigree, but unlike Brittany, it preserves very little of the Celtic language that was originally spoken there. The region is named for the Gallaeci, the Celtic-speaking people who lived in northwestern Iberia in the 1st millennium BC. The Romans conquered them during the reign of Augustus, around the turn of the 1st and 2nd millennia.

- They were ruled by Rome thereafter until 410 AD, when the Germanic tribe known as the Suebi settled in the region. The Suebi in turn were conquered by another Germanic people, the Visigoths, who established hegemony over all of Spain in the 5th century.

- Like Brittany, Galicia also received an infusion of Celtic speakers from Britain in the 5th century, at just the time that other groups of people from western Britain were settling in Brittany. However, there was a key difference between Galicia and Brittany. Unlike in Brittany, where the newcomers provided a kind of Celtic transfusion, in Galicia, the newcomers did not lead to the establishment and preservation of a Celtic language as the local vernacular.

- The reason was that by the period of the British migrations, the Celtic character of Iberia was already severely attenuated. The Iberian Peninsula was more thoroughly Romanized than Gaul. Moreover, Spain had not been entirely Celtic speaking at the time of the Roman conquest. Linguistic diversity probably hastened the transition in Roman-ruled Iberia to the Latin language.

- By the 5th century, the Celtic languages that had been spoken in Spain had declined precipitously. Thus, when the British speakers arrived in Galicia, there was less of a Celtic language base on which to build, and their influence ultimately dissipated. The local language spoken in Galicia today is on the dialect continuum between Spanish and Portuguese.

Spanish and Irish Connections

- One of the most intriguing aspects of Galicia for Celtic enthusiasts comes from the intriguing hints of a connection between Spain and Ireland. The main text about Irish origins, *The Book of Invasions*, claims that the inhabitants of Ireland came from Spain. However, it's not particularly likely these stories are true.

- Regardless, a theory positing that the Celtic languages may have arisen on the Atlantic coast of Europe does present some interesting possibilities. From the few linguistic clues that survive about the Galician Celtic language, it seems to have been a Q-Celtic version of Celtic. Irish is also Q-Celtic, whereas the Celtic languages of Britain are P-Celtic. Gaulish was probably P-Celtic as well.

- This would tend to suggest that Celtic made it to Ireland from Spain. Perhaps some anonymous traders deep in the remote past brought Celtic to Ireland from Galicia.

- We have no evidence that the story of a Spanish origin for the Irish was known in Spain in the early Middle Ages, but it did become widely known many centuries later. Now, the Spanish are very conscious of the existence of this story, leading to a big tourist business.

- An example is a monument on the Galician coast in A Coruña that has been interpreted as the Tower of Breógan. (It is actually a Roman lighthouse.) A modern statue of Breógan has been placed at the start of the pathway to the tower, greeting visitors as they approach from the parking lot. Breógan was a character in *The Book of Invasions* who supposedly built a tower from which his sons were able to spot the island of Ireland.

- Additionally, Galician music has many affinities with music in other parts of the Celtic Fringe. Even if Galicians don't have a viable Celtic language, they do

Breógan

have music that sounds Celtic, and they may just be able to claim that they helped to turn Ireland Celtic several thousand years ago. Galicia is certainly making every effort to get into the Celtic club. Its Celtic status seems to have been widely accepted by both scholars and, more lucratively, tourists.

Suggested Reading

Cunliffe, *Facing the Ocean*, chapters 5 and 10.

Galliou and Jones, *The Bretons*.

Geoffrey of Monmouth, *The History of the Kings of Britain*.

Gillingham, *The Angevin Empire*, chapter 5.

Questions to Consider

1. How did the Celtic legacy in Brittany and Galicia differ from the Celtic legacy in other parts of the Celtic Fringe?

2. In what ways have inhabitants of Brittany and Galicia made use of their Celtic past for political purposes?

Lecture 12

Celtic Churches

This lecture focuses on the way Christianity was brought to the Celtic lands, particularly Ireland. The lecture tries to answer the question of what, if anything, was Celtic about Christianity in the Celtic world. It used to be thought that a fair bit of Celtic paganism was preserved in Celtic Christianity, and it also used to be thought that there was a major fault-line in the Celtic church between those who favored this Celtic-flavored Christianity and those who wanted to stay more in line with the Christian Church elsewhere in Europe. Scholars are far less sure about this now than they used to be.

Christianity in the Celtic Lands

- The first of the Celtic areas to be Christianized that we know of was Roman Britain. We have evidence for Christianity in Roman Britain from as early as the 3rd century AD, possibly slightly earlier. It's certainly possible that Christianity reached Brittany and Galicia around the same time, but we can't be sure.

- Since Britain was very tightly connected to Gaul at the time, the presumption is that missionaries from Gaul brought the Christian faith to Britain, where it first took root in the urban areas and then spread out into the countryside. From the main areas of Roman control in Britain in the southeast, Christianity spread to the north and west, and most likely from there to Ireland, probably as early as the late 4th century.

- In the case of Ireland, though, the first people to bring Christianity may have been not missionaries but Christian slaves brought to Ireland against their will. This was also a period when some Irish dynasties, particularly in the south and east of Ireland, were establishing branches in western Britain, and they may well have come in contact with Christians there and brought the faith back.

- However it spread, there were enough Christians in Ireland that in 431, Pope Celestine sent a bishop named Palladius from Gaul to Ireland to minister to "the Irish believing in Christ." The Christian community by this point must have numbered in the hundreds at least, and it must have been vocal enough to be heard all the way in Rome.

- Palladius duly went to Ireland, and he seems to have had several disciples as well. They founded churches, mostly in the southeast. We know very little about their work, unfortunately, because no written sources about their mission survive.

- That is emphatically not the case for another very important traveler to Ireland: St. Patrick. St. Patrick was a Romano-British youth who was captured by Irish raiders and brought to Ireland, where he served his master for six years by tending sheep, probably in the northern part of Ireland. While he was alone with the sheep, he received a divine call to escape from captivity, become a priest, and return to convert the Irish. That's what he did.

- Because Ireland was a very decentralized place, with many small independent kingdoms, St. Patrick had to go around preaching to all of these kingdoms individually. St. Patrick also had to battle against some important social and cultural presuppositions in Irish society.

- St. Patrick evidently preached a fairly pacifist brand of Christianity. This emphasis on peace was a tough sell in Ireland, where fighting was endemic and likely necessary since there was no developed state to protect people from their enemies.

- The other problem St. Patrick had in preaching Christianity had to do with marriage. The Christian establishment in its early centuries was profoundly ambivalent towards marriage. At best, it regarded marriage as a lesser option after virginity.

- St. Patrick apparently preached the value of virginity to his converts, and the idea did not go over well with their parents. Irish society was based on kinship, and in this system, marriages were very important for establishing relationships with potential political and military allies, and for producing offspring. St. Patrick's converts apparently faced tremendous parental pressure to renounce their new faith due to this issue of marriage.

- Many of St. Patrick's new Christians did marry, and his work bore fruit, along with that of probably many other missionaries whose names we do not know. At some point in the early 5th century, other missionaries brought the monastic movement to Ireland, possibly from both southwestern Scotland and Wales.

- Monasteries became very important centers of learning in Ireland. The decentralized nature of monastic churches fit very well with the Irish political landscape.

St. Brigid

- One of the most famous monastic figures in early Irish history was St. Brigid. There has been tremendous scholarly controversy over the last few decades about St. Brigid. We have three biographies of Brigid that survive from the 7th and 8th centuries, of which two are in Latin and one is in Old Irish.

- Brigid was born in around 451 AD as the daughter of a chieftain from Leinster in eastern Ireland and a Christian slave who may have been a Pictish captive converted by St. Patrick. She eventually established a monastic house at Kildare.

- The earliest of the three biographies of Brigid makes her look like a pretty standard (if powerful) Christian saint, but the next two include a lot of material that makes her look a bit pre-Christian. In these texts, Brigid could control the waters of Ireland's rivers, among other elemental powers.

- These texts have led some scholars to theorize that Brigid was not a real person at all, but a goddess figure who had been recast as a

Christian saint. This course's view is that Brigid was likely a real (albeit embellished) person, but we can't be sure. The main point to take away from the story of St. Brigid is that early Irish Christianity had more than a small share of pagan elements blended into it.

- The most important aspect of St. Brigid's career was certainly her work as a monastic leader. Monasticism in Ireland was very ascetic; it emphasized the mortification of the flesh to purge the monk of worldly desires. Monks ate very sparse diets, and most monks initially lived in very simple huts made of perishable materials that no longer survive, but slightly later they began building in stone.

- There was also a great stress on pilgrimage, on the willing sacrifice of the comforts of home and family in order to get closer to God. There were three main areas where Irish monastic pilgrims went. They could go far as continental Europe. They could also go to other locations closer to home, such as the various parts of the British Isles. Or they might simply abandon themselves to the open sea.

Networks

- Irish monks also established networks of monasteries that flourished for centuries. The two most important figures in this movement were named St. Columba and St. Columbanus. St. Columba is notable for founding a very important confederation of monasteries all over the northern half of Ireland and southwestern Scotland, including Derry, Durrow, and Kells.

- The most famous was Iona, which was situated on an island in southwestern Scotland. Iona ultimately provided the missionaries who converted the northern half of Britain, so it had a huge influence throughout the British Isles.

- St. Columbanus was born in about 543 AD and died in 615. He set out for Gaul with 12 followers and was a genuinely ascetic man, but he was also a difficult one. He insisted on speaking truth to power, in this case, the king of the Franks, who had taken over Gaul by this point, and for whom France is named. St. Columbanus criticized King Theudebert II for his lax sexual morals.

- Columbanus also followed a different method for calculating the date of Easter. The Frankish clerics would not tolerate this difference of opinion, so he was exiled from the Frankish court. This proved to be a good thing for European culture, because he went on to found important houses all over France and northern Italy that helped preserve the learning of antiquity.

Seagoing Pilgrims

- As previously mentioned, some pilgrims set out to sea with the deliberate aim of letting the wind take them wherever it would. Some monks returned to tell marvelous stories about what they had seen.

- The most famous such tale is the *Voyage of St. Brendan*. St. Brendan was a monk who supposedly set out with his companions to find the so-called Isles of the Saints. After many adventures, including an encounter with an island that turned out to be a whale and a narrow escape from an island that spewed fire, he reached his goal.

- Many people have read this story as a description of a trans-Atlantic voyage to Newfoundland, and in the 1970s, the explorer Tim

Severin actually reconstructed the hide-covered boat that St. Brendan would have used and demonstrated that such a voyage would have been possible.

- However, there are two possible reasons to suspect the tales of St. Brendan. One is that they might have an allegorical Christian meaning: This was not a real sea voyage but the voyage of the soul toward God. The other reason is that they resemble secular Irish tales about journeys to the Otherworld across the sea. But we do know that some monks really went on such voyages; this was a distinctive feature of Christianity in Ireland.

The Broader Christian World

- What was the relationship between the Celtic churches and the western Christian establishment as a whole? The idea of Christian distinctiveness arose because there were some genuine differences between the way Christianity was practiced in the areas of Celtic speech and in the more Roman-oriented areas of England in the south and east, but they tended to concern questions of ritual observance rather than actual belief.

- For example, monks marked their monastic status by cutting their hair in a special way. This was known as the tonsure, which comes from a Latin word for barbering. But the form of the tonsure was different in Ireland compared to elsewhere.

- Most monks would shave a round patch on the top of their heads and cut their remaining hair short all around. This is the Roman tonsure, the tonsure that most people are familiar with today. In Ireland, the tonsure was quite different. Men would shave their heads from the top forward and then leave the rest of the hair long.

- Another issue touched on actual liturgical practice: the question of when to celebrate Easter. Easter is a movable feast; it's not tied to a specific date on the calendar like Christmas, but rather to the relationship between the spring equinox and the phases of the moon.

- Early on, Christians changed their minds several times about exactly how to reckon the date of Easter. One of our earliest pieces of evidence for the date when Christianity started to make headway in Ireland is a piece of an old Easter table that reflects the method of calculating Easter from the late 4th century, so we know that Christianity probably got to Ireland before St. Patrick arrived there in the 5th century.

- The church changed its mind twice more in the following two centuries, but not everybody went along with the second change. By the 7th century, all the Christian churches had adopted the second change except for the Irish and some of the British. Increasingly, the discrepancy bothered people.

- The Irish churches of the south got together in the year 631 and decided to conform, but most of the northern Irish churches held out. The same geographic split between north and south also held on the island of Britain, because northern England in particular was largely Christianized by Irish missionaries from Iona who used the older date of Easter. Meanwhile, in the south of England, they were using the newer date of Easter that had been introduced in Rome.

- Things might have carried on this way in both Ireland and Britain. However, in the 660s, the Northumbrian king, Oswiu, was married to a princess from another part of England where they used the Roman Easter. Husband and wife each followed the Easter they were used to. That meant that sometimes when spring rolled around, it would still be Lent for the queen, so she would still be fasting, but Easter would have already arrived for the king, so he would be feasting. That didn't work so well at court.

- In 664, a meeting was held called the Synod of Whitby, at which the king got his advisers together and they decided once and for all to use the Roman Easter. This meant that England was going to orient itself much more toward the continent than toward Ireland, so Irish influence in England diminished.

- Scholars have recently cast some doubt on the traditional story of the Synod of Whitby. Almost everything we know about the synod comes from a book written by a Northumbrian monk (that is, an English-speaking monk) named the Venerable Bede. In the 720s and 730s, Bede wrote the *Ecclesiastical History of the English People*, and we can confidently state that Bede was biased toward the English.

- Bede tended to create a very stark dichotomy between Roman Christianity on the one hand and the Christianity of the Irish and British on the other. But it is easy to exaggerate these differences. They irritated people at the time, but probably not as much as we might think.

- We should keep in mind that the Christian church before the Synod of Whitby had been convulsed multiple times by serious, even fundamental disagreements on core aspects of Christian doctrine, such as the relationship between the Father and the Son within the Holy Trinity. None of the issues that were supposedly debated at Whitby are as serious as these other theological questions. That doesn't mean they were not serious distractions at the time, but we should resist the idea that they represent some kind of distinctive Celtic Christianity.

Suggested Readings

Adomnan of Iona, *Life of St. Columba*.
Bede, *Ecclesiastical History*, book 3, chapter 25.
Bitel, *Isle of the Saints*.
———, "St. Brigid of Ireland."
Cahill, *How the Irish Saved Civiliziation*.
O'Meara, trans., *The Voyage of Saint Brendan*.
Skinner, trans., *The Confession of Saint Patrick and Letter to Coroticus*.

Questions to Consider

1. How distinctive were the Celtic churches?

2. How did the conversion of Ireland to Christianity affect its relationship with the wider world?

Lecture 13

Celtic Art and Insular Art

Irish art of the early Middle Ages is one of the most popular manifestations of the Celtic phenomenon. Artifacts like the *Book of Kells* draw hundreds of thousands of visitors each year, and motifs from the *Book of Kells* can be found on just about everything with a surface, from clothing and jewelry to housewares and beyond. This lecture looks at the spread of Celtic-style art from the continent to the British Isles and Ireland before the coming of Christianity, and then looks at what happened to this art in the early Christian period.

Book of Kells

Fascination

- The fascination with Irish art dates from the 19th century, when the idea that there was a distinctive Celtic style of art first arose. At that point, scholars looked at the art of Ireland and the British Isles in the early Middle Ages and identified certain elements that seemed to set this art apart from other art styles. By this point, the idea of the Celts as a distinctive people with their own language and culture was well advanced, so it made sense to extend the concept to art.

- This was a period of spectacular archaeological finds, both on the European continent and in Britain and Ireland. The scholars who studied these finds assumed that the people who produced these artifacts were all Celts. This is a somewhat problematic notion; the people who produced this art had no idea that anyone would ever label it as Celtic. For example, the people who originated the La Tène art style we associate with the Celts may not have been Celtic speakers at all.

- This style arguably reached its most sophisticated development on the fringes of the area where it was originally popular, in what we think of now as the Celtic Fringe. It is this late flowering of the Celtic art style, in the late Iron Age and early Christian period, that this lecture focuses on.

Terminology and Background

- When talking about Celtic art in the British Isles and Ireland, scholars are faced with the difficulty of deciding whether a particular work was made in Ireland or Britain because there was such a broad similarity all across this region among artifacts produced in this style. Thus, scholars often refer to this art style in one of two ways.

- If they're talking about the period after the Germanic migrations to Britain, they might call this art Hiberno-Saxon, which suggests that the art style is a blend of Irish and English elements. But it is more common to use an even more general term and simply call it *insular* art, from the fact that it was produced on an island: perhaps Ireland, perhaps Britain, and perhaps an unknowable island. Insular art is Celtic-style art in Britain and Ireland.

- Recall the art found at the La Tène site in Switzerland discussed in a previous lecture. This is a very stylized art. The figures are not intended to be realistic; they are meant to suggest the figures, not represent them. This art also emphasizes repeating patterns and abstract elements; sometimes these are geometric, but often they are curvilinear, with spiral forms and interlacing forms.

- This art style became wildly popular in large parts of Europe, including Central Europe and Gaul, but it was only represented in a very scattered way in Spain. In fact, the areas where this art were popular were in some cases cut off from each other by land.

- Thus, the style probably had to have been spread at least partly by sea, likely due to trading contacts up and down the Atlantic coast of Europe. Trading contacts probably brought the La Tène style to Britain and Ireland sometime in the centuries right before Christ.

- The art we see in Britain and Ireland is subtly different from what we see on the continent. The motifs are very similar, but they are produced in slightly different ways, much more as if native craftspeople in Britain were copying work that they had seen, possibly on objects brought by traders.

- The similarity in art is not a sign of some kind of genetic connection between the continent and the British Isles; it is merely a sign that this art style proved enormously popular in certain parts of the British Isles. Strikingly, this art was a survivor while the style on continental Europe was swept away by the Roman conquest of Gaul. Very little of the earlier La Tène style can be found after the 1st century AD.

- The original art style from La Tène blended elements from the many areas with which the peoples of Central Europe had trading contacts.

Influences include Celtic motifs and Germanic art, with its strong emphasis on certain animal shapes.

● Another important influence on this art style was classical art from the Mediterranean area, which brought in certain vegetal motifs, like the acanthus leaf, as well as broad-ribbon interlace. This art had come into the picture largely due to the influence of Christian missionaries.

Metalworking

● This lecture turns now to specific examples of the techniques used to make art, starting with metalworking. The techniques and motifs of early Irish metalwork seem to have come about in the 3rd and 4th centuries due to trading contacts between Ireland and Roman Britain.

● Almost everything that survives in metalwork from early Ireland is related to religion in some way. Reliquaries and altar vessels were the most common, but there were also items like bells and bishop's crosiers. Brooches were a notable exception. Probably the most famous liturgical object to survive from this period is the Ardagh Chalice, which is on display in Dublin in the National Museum of Ireland.

Ardagh Chalice

● Reliquaries survive in relatively large numbers. A reliquary is a vessel meant to contain a relic, which is an object associated with a saint. In Ireland, we have a lot of them dating especially to the 7th through the 9th centuries. They could be of various sizes, depending on whether they were supposed to be for personal or communal use.

- A secular object is perhaps the single most famous metal artifact of early Christian Ireland, namely, the Tara Brooch. Brooches were extremely important in Irish society because they were vital to keeping clothes on; buttons or zippers weren't in use.

- The Tara Brooch is a spectacular example. It is decorated with exquisite gold filigree triple spirals, scrolls, and animal motifs. The Tara brooch was dug up in the middle of the 19th century in the village of Bettystown in 1850. It was a sensation. Queen Victoria loved it so much that she gave several replicas as gifts.

Manuscripts

Book of Kells

- Manuscripts, like reliquaries, brooches, and liturgical vessels, came in all different levels of ornamentation. Some were clearly very basic, intended for practical use. They may have contained few if any illustrations.

- Scholars tend to focus on the most elaborately decorated manuscripts that come from the *scriptoria* (or writing rooms) of the richest religious houses. They have survived disproportionately because they are so beautiful and they were treated with special care over the centuries.

- These manuscripts contain motifs that are very similar to those found

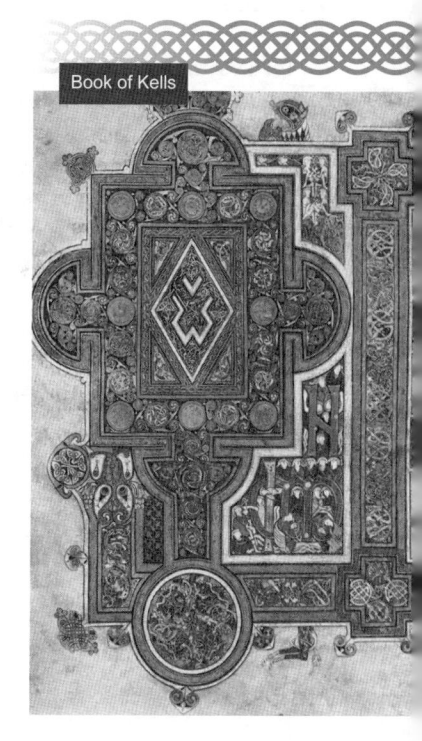

The Celtic World | 129

in metalworking—such as various animal shapes and interwoven patterns—but they are two-dimensional representations of a three-dimensional process. It's as if the manuscripts are trying to represent objects and motifs that people would have been familiar with from their daily experience.

- The highpoint of the insular style with regard to manuscripts occupied a narrow range in time, roughly from the late 7th to the early 9th century. We're not sure exactly why the style tended to fade away. There are theories, but we can't be certain. Key examples of this style include the *Book of Kells* and the *Lindisfarne Gospels*.

Textiles

- Textiles were a particularly ubiquitous medium. People who could produce high-quality textiles were very highly regarded in this society. The most prestigious garments were those that had been elaborately embroidered, almost always by women. In the Irish system of setting the rate of compensation to be paid for injuring people of different social and occupational status, the honor price of an embroideress was higher than that of a queen.

- Unfortunately, textiles don't survive very well in the Irish climate, so we don't really know what these elaborately embroidered garments looked like. However, given the very strong continuities between the motifs used in various art forms in insular art, we can certainly speculate that luxury textiles in the insular world were embroidered with motifs that are familiar to us from the great insular manuscripts. The elaborate embroidery that we see on, say, modern Irish dancing costumes may well represent a throwback to a genuine elite tradition from early Ireland.

Stone Carving

- We know less about the medium of stone carving than we do about manuscripts or metalwork because it has often suffered from exposure to the elements, and it can be harder to pin it down to precise dates than it is for manuscripts in particular. It's worth looking at stone carving, though, because even if we can't date every item precisely, it is possible to trace the development of various forms in relative terms.

- The earliest stone carvings that survive are simply inscriptions in a distinctive alphabet known as Ogham, in which the letters are formed by groups of horizontal or diagonal strokes on a central baseline, often formed from the side of a standing stone. These inscriptions, which date from the 4th to the 6th centuries, were mostly grave markers.

- As Ireland became more and more Christianized, these stones developed into Christian gravestones, and Latin letters replaced Ogham. These gravestones either stood upright or were lying on the ground. For example, there is a grave slab from the important monastery of Clonmacnoise dating from the 8th century that is inscribed with a prayer for Tuathal the craftsman. The prayer is written to follow around the arms of the cross.

- The most famous stone sculptures are spectacular high crosses. The origins of the high crosses are disputed, as they seem to have evolved in Ireland and Britain virtually simultaneously around the 8th century. There was a lot of contact back and forth between the two islands.

- These crosses have a characteristic nimbus or circle around the crosspoint of the two shafts. This nimbus may have represented the celestial sphere, but it could also have had the practical function of helping to sustain the arms of the cross. Crosses with nimbuses became enormously popular in the Gaelic revival movement of the 19th century, when it was first called the Celtic cross.

132 | Lecture 13 ⬢ Celtic Art and Insular Art

- These crosses were the sites of the same kind of intricate interlace motifs as the metalwork and manuscript illumination. Later, crosses began to depict Biblical figures, as in the Ahenny Cross, which shows David bringing the defeated Goliath back to Jerusalem.

- One of the most spectacular examples is the 10th-century *Cross of the Scriptures* from Clonmacnoise. The crucifixion of Jesus is depicted at the center. At Clonmacnoise today, the version displayed outside is a copy; the original is too precious to be displayed outdoors, so it is kept in a museum.

Suggested Readings

Farley and Hunter, *Celts: Art and Identity*, chapter 8.
Megaw and Megaw, *Celtic Art*, pp. 243–57.
Nordenfalk, *Celtic and Anglo-Saxon Painting*.

Questions to Consider

1. In what ways did insular art perpetuate the art of the La Tène period, and in what ways did it depart from it?

2. What can insular art tell us about the values of the society that produced it?

Lecture 14

Medieval Irish Literature

This lecture focuses on the very rich subject of early Irish literature. The medieval Irish wrote copiously in Latin; however, the factor that sets them apart from every other people in Europe in the early Middle Ages is that they wrote prolifically in their own language. The Irish produced the largest body of medieval texts not just in any Celtic language but in any vernacular language whatsoever. For the period before the year 1000, there are hundreds of medieval Irish stories, compared to a few tales and fragments in French or German. And the literature that survives is rich and varied. That vernacular literary phenomenon is a large point of interest for this lecture.

The Importance of Medieval Irish Literature

- In early Irish society, the highest grade of poets had the status of kings. They had the same honor price as a king or a bishop; that is, an offending party had to pay the same very high amount to compensate their kin if they were injured or killed. Poets were some of the only people who could move freely throughout the countryside without needing to ask permission to enter a new territory.

- Early Irish kings and later clan chiefs commissioned poets to sing their praises. This was a society that functioned on reputation. Status was delineated not just by how many cattle a person had, but also on how skilled a poet one could employ to boast about them.

- The flip side of praise poetry was satire; a satirist might have been employed to make their patron's enemies look bad. The profession of satirist doesn't seem to have been limited to males. In the epic called the *Táin*, there is a woman satirist named Leborcham, and people are terrified of her.

Traits of Irish Literature

- Irish literature has a very distinctive feel to it. The plots are one distinctive feature. Until rather recently, most plots in the broader European literary tradition were fairly linear in structure. Irish stories, however, can be full of digressions, and in some cases the digressions threaten to overwhelm the plot.

- Another noticeable feature of Irish literature is that it tends to fall into very specific genres. In fact, we have several surviving tale lists from the Middle Ages that put the early Irish tales into these categories. For example, the Irish had a category called "the death of kings," which lived up to its name.

- The multitude of medieval classifications for these tales can be somewhat unwieldy to work with. Instead, modern scholars have grouped these tales into four big cycles that are distinguished more by subject matter rather than by tale type. There is more than one tale type in each cycle.

- The four big cycles, in roughly chronological order, are as follows:

  1. The mythological cycle, which covers the peopling of Ireland and the early clashes between the early inhabitants and various supernatural beings.

  2. The Ulster cycle, which deals with the conflict between two provinces of Ireland, Ulster and Connacht. It is especially prominent in the great cattle raid that is the subject of the *Táin*.

  3. The king tales, which take place during the early centuries after the conversion of Ireland to Christianity; some of these are probably based on real events, even if only very loosely.

  4. The Ossian cycle, which are tales that take place in the later medieval period concerning the great warrior Finn MacCool and his band of companions as well as Finn's son Ossian.

- This lecture discusses the first three cycles. The fourth is covered in a later lecture on the discovery of the Celts in early modern Europe.

The Mythological Cycle

- The mythological cycle is important for scholars for various reasons. This is one of the only places we can look to try to recover something of pre-Christian Irish religion or mythology. The tales take place in a distant, pre-Christian past, and they include many supernatural elements.

- One of the most important threads in this cycle includes the stories of the peopling of Ireland that came to be known as the *Lebor Gabala Erenn*, or *The Book of Invasions*. Two closely related tales from this tradition can give a good sense of this material.

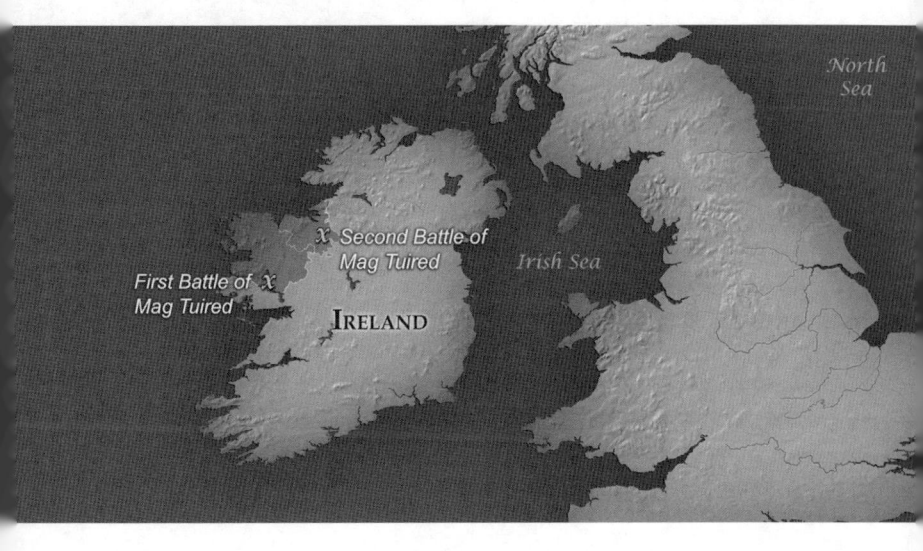

- The two tales are called "The First Battle of Mag Tuired" and "The Second Battle of Mag Tuired." The first is set near Cong in County Mayo, and the second is set by Lough Arrow in County Sligo. We are told that the people known as the Nemedians have left Ireland in three separate groups to escape the Fomorian giants.

* First, one of these groups, the Fir Bolg, returns to Ireland from exile in Greece and conquers the Fomorians, but then a second group, known as the Tuatha Dé Danann, arrives. Under the leadership of their king, Nuada, the Tuatha arrive in Ireland to demand that the Fir Bolg either face them in battle or concede half of the island to them.

* The choice is for battle, and Nuada ends up facing the champion of the Fir Bolg, a man named Sreng. Sreng cuts off Nuada's right hand, but the Tuatha win the battle. The Fir Bolg are confined to the province of Connacht, leaving the rest of the island to the Tuatha.

* One of the Tuatha, Dian Cecht, who is a god of healing, gives Nuada a new, artificial hand. However, a complicated factor emerges: Kings cannot have any physical blemishes, because they need to represent the integrity of the people. For seven years, the Tuatha are ruled by a different king named Bres, who is part Tuatha, part Fomorian giant. Once Bres dies, Nuada's arm is restored, and he is put back on the throne.

Fir Bolg and Tuath Dé

* In the ensuing tale of the second battle, Bres is more of a villain. His Fomorian ancestry causes him to oppress the Tuatha. Bres is deposed, and Nuada's flesh regrows over his silver arm, so he is restored to the throne.

138 | Lecture 14 ☸ Medieval Irish Literature

- The big difference between the stories is that in the first story, Nuada is restored because Bres dies, but in the second story, Bres is deposed, so he leads a counterrevolution with the help of a Fomorian named Balor. In the ensuing battle, Nuada is killed, but a new Tuatha champion named Lugh is triumphant.

- Bres survives, and his life is spared on the condition that he teach the Tuatha how to farm, which he does. These are fundamentally tales about the right way to rule. Kings who do not meet their subjects' expectations can expect to face a challenge.

The Ulster Cycle

- If the mythological cycle takes place at some sort of early phase of the settlement of Ireland, the Ulster cycle belongs to a slightly more recognizable but still pre-Christian past. The most famous story of this cycle is the *Táin*. The *Táin* has heroes, the most important of which by far is Cú Chulainn. He is the son of a woman named Deichtine, herself the daughter of Ulster's king, Conchobar. Cú Chulainn's father is the god Lugh.

- Cú Chulainn has a unique appearance, featuring multicolored hair and seven-digit hands and toes, "the nails or claws or talons of each with the grip of a hawk or a griffin." His eyes have gems in them. When his battle rage is on him, he goes into what translators have variously called his "warp-spasm" or "torque," which is some kind of frightening contortion that has a dramatic effect on an already unusual-looking young man.

- Alongside Cu Chulainn, the most compelling character in the *Táin* is undoubtedly Medb, the queen of Connacht. It is Medb who starts off the whole story of the cattle raid because she is jealous of her husband's bull. She seems to be descended from a goddess figure linked to sovereignty and intoxication.

- The Ulster cycle ends with the victory of the Ulstermen over Connacht, but in the process, huge slaughter is done on both sides, and the bull is killed. Medb's jealousy has had terrible consequences. Cú Chulainn tries in vain to avoid fighting his foster brother Ferdia, but he cannot do so without shame, and so he chooses to kill Ferdia, but his heart is broken.

The King Tales

- The third cycles involves the tales of the Irish kings. These tales take place in an ancient Christianized Ireland. There is still a lot of mythological material, and it's clear that the transition to Christianity has not been seamless. The reason these tales are so important is that they have a serious point to make about the proper exercise of kingship in Ireland. The tales look at kingship in two parts of a king's life cycle: when a king takes the throne, and when he dies.

- One of the most important Irish myths is the myth of the goddess of sovereignty. The goddess of sovereignty was the embodiment of the right to rule, and it was the goddess who conveyed this right on individual rulers.

- In this story, we have a familiar situation in Irish literature: There is a king's son who is trying to make his way in the world, but he is the youngest in a large family of brothers, and moreover, his mother is not the official wife of the king, but rather a servant of lower status. He has something to prove. The name of the youngest brother is Niall.

- One day, he is out with his older half-brothers, and they come across an old woman. She offers them a drink from her well, but she is only willing to give them the water if they will pay a small price. She wants a kiss.

- None of the other brothers want to kiss her, but the youngest leaps at the opportunity. He says that not only will he kiss her; he will lie with her as well. He demonstrates his good faith, and at that moment, the old woman is transformed into a beautiful young woman, and presumably only after the transformation does Niall have to carry through on his promise.

- It turns out that the woman represents the sovereignty of Ireland. Niall does go on to become king. In fact, he becomes the very famous king known as Niall of the Nine Hostages. In Ireland, this story had a very important political meaning. The idea was that sovereignty was hard to acquire but beautiful to keep. For the Irish, stories of this kind were deeply political. Literature in Ireland was never just for entertainment.

- People in early Ireland were sophisticated consumers of these literary traditions. They could recognize a good allegory when they saw one. They did not believe that the goddess literally chose the successful claimant for the throne. But these stories about the sovereignty goddess helped to ratify the results of what could be an extremely messy and even bloody process.

- Many stories of the sovereignty goddess are about acquiring the throne, but a lot of them are also about losing the throne. These fall into the enormous death-of-kings genre. The most famous of these is *The Destruction of Da Derga's Hostel*, in which an unjust king is punished for violating his responsibility to provide equal justice to his subjects.

- In this story, King Conaire is promised that if he avoids violating certain *geasa*, or taboos, such as not allowing three redheaded men to precede him into the house of a redheaded man, he will be a successful king. Conaire rules justly, and as a result, the land flourishes. But Conaire has a problem: his foster brothers.

- They are criminals, and Conaire is caught between his duty to punish wrongdoers and his personal obligation to his foster brothers. Rather than treat them as they deserve, he merely banishes them, but they continue to raid Conaire's kingdom. As a result, the good omens of Conaire's early reign are reversed. The weather worsens, and the crops wither.

- Conaire is forced repeatedly to violate the *geasa* that he was told he must not violate. Conaire is drawn into a final battle against the marauders, and he is killed. When faced with a moral dilemma, he chooses incorrectly, and the story punishes him for it.

Suggested Readings

Carson, trans., *The Táin*.

Cross and Slover, *Ancient Irish Tales*.

Dillon and Chadwick, *The Celtic Realms*, chapter 10.

Gantz, trans., *Early Irish Myths and Sagas*.

Hoagland, *1,000 Years of Irish Poetry*.

Koch and Carey, *The Celtic Heroic Age*, pp. 51–282.

McCone, *Pagan Past and Christian Present in Early Irish Literature*.

Rees and Rees, *Celtic Heritage*.

Questions to Consider

1. What can early Irish literature tell us about the values of the society that produced it?

2. How is early Irish literature distinct from modern western literary traditions?

Lecture 15

Celtic Women, Families, and Social Structure

This lecture discusses the society of the Celtic lands in the early Middle Ages. Topics include societal organization, distinctive institutions, and the role of families. Law and lawyers are also of particular interest, owing to the importance of law in Celtic society and the prevalence of surviving legal texts. The lecture also looks at the role of women in Celtic societies, a topic that has received quite a bit of attention from scholars and from the general public in recent years.

Four Traits: A Tribal Society

- The historian Daniel Binchy claimed in 1954 that early Ireland was "tribal, rural, hierarchical and familiar." This statement has been refined and criticized since, but this course's view is that it's essentially true, and it's a useful way of organizing the information. (It largely applies to Wales as well.) Following is a breakdown of this four-fold schema.

- By "tribal," Binchy meant that Ireland was composed of many small units or kingdoms, probably at least 100 at any one time. Besides these tiny kingdoms, Ireland was also very loosely divided into bigger units called provinces. They were not concrete political entities; they were more like geographical ideas.

- There were at various points four or five of these provinces. Today, there are four: Ulster is in the north, Connacht in the west, Leinster in the southeast, and Munster in the southwest. The middle province was called Meath, which means "middle," but it has been absorbed by the other four.

- There were no political entities that covered the whole country. Thus, a person's political loyalty would have been very localized indeed. It would be determined by one's relationship to the king or *rí* of their own *túath*, and that might be a group of only a few thousand people.

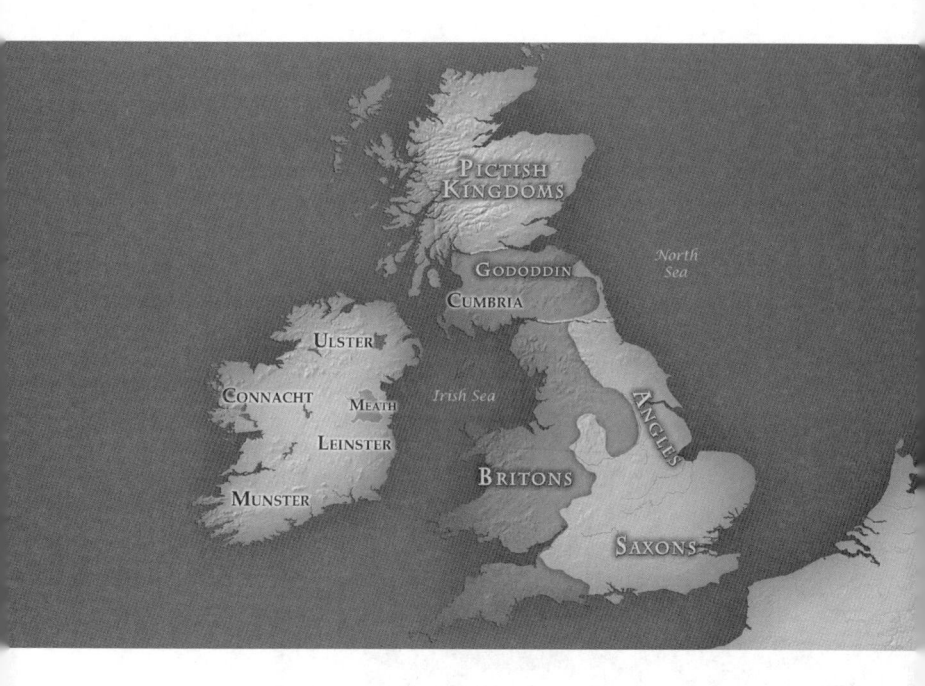

A Rural Society

- There were no cities at all in early Ireland. This is the second part of Binchy's definition: that Ireland is rural. This was not as true for some of the other Celtic-speaking areas as it was for Ireland. In Ireland, people lived in widely scattered settlements, either in homesteads where there was an enclosure—if they were somewhat wealthy—or simply in isolated farms.

- In Ireland the enclosures are usually called ringforts, though they weren't really forts since they were not usually placed on the highest ground available. The most common type of ringfort was called the *ráth*. A bank and an impressive outer ditch surrounded it. Occasionally there were two or more walls, usually made of earth. The enclosures were not huge; a typical diameter was 100 feet.

- Another type of ringfort, the *caiseal*, was built with stone. These were mostly built in the west where the landscape is rockier. They had drystone walls, usually without ditches. An additional type of building was the *dún*, a more elaborate stone structure, often with separate concentric stone rings. These may have been intended for defense.

- A final type of dwelling was the *crannog*. It was, by definition, found on an island in a lake. This is a very old tradition in Ireland that goes back to the late Bronze Age and continued well into the Christian period, but there is a modern reconstruction in County Clare.

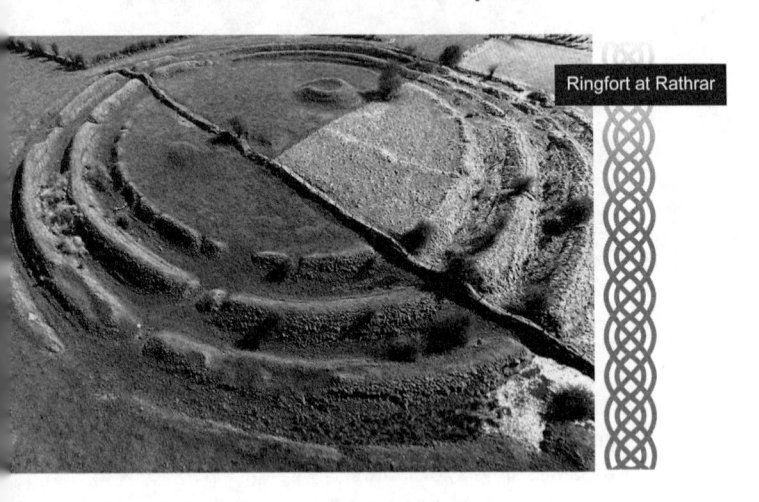

Ringfort at Rathrar

A Familiar Society

- By calling Ireland familiar, Binchy meant it was a family-centered society. The family, not the individual, was the basic unit of Irish society. There was a precise definition of the family for legal purposes. It was called the *fine*, or "kin group," and it extended to more or fewer members depending on the particular situation involved.

- Belonging to a *fine* gave a person rights, such as the ability to inherit land within the group. But it also brought responsibilities. The kin group had to consult each other about the distribution or sale of property and also stand with each other in the face of legal disputes.

- A *fine* was often given the specific name *derbfine*, which literally meant "certain kin." This meant all the relatives who went back to a common great-grandfather, so four generations. This was the usual group that would be involved in inheriting land and property. A married woman belonged to the *derbfine* of her husband.

- The Irish legal system was entirely based on what we would think of as civil law rather than criminal law. In other words, it was all about the lawsuit. People sued each other for things that would be considered criminal offenses today, like murder and assault.

- These matters were handled as private transactions between the parties, but it was the two kin groups who settled the dispute, not the two individuals. The losing party in the suit would go to their relatives to help pay the damages owed to the winner. A person's contribution was prorated based on the closeness of their relationship to the offender. This was a real incentive to keep difficult family members in line.

- A family could be extended by the institution of fosterage, in which children were raised by another family, sometimes from quite early ages. This often resulted in lifelong ties of friendship that could be very useful in economic and political relationships later in life.

A Hierarchical Society

- The final characteristic of Irish society is that it was hierarchical. Families varied greatly in status, as they did in many medieval societies. Much of a person's daily existence was determined by where they stood in this hierarchy. This status was fixed according to two main criteria: wealth and occupation.

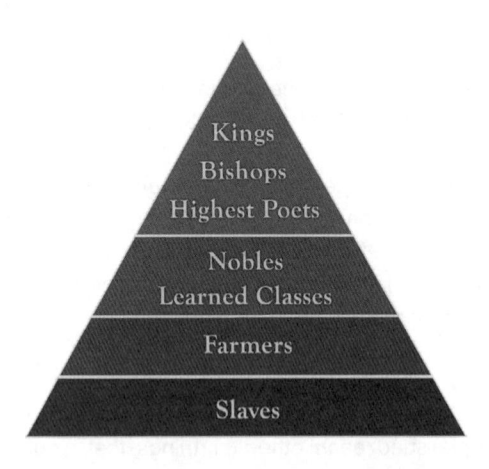

Pyramid diagram:
- Kings / Bishops / Highest Poets
- Nobles / Learned Classes
- Farmers
- Slaves

- The social status of the victim determined the price kin groups had to help pay for injuries inflicted by their members. The more important they were, the more a group had to pay for injuring them. The price was expressed in a unit called the *cumal*, which was worth either one slave girl or three cows.

- The price was meant to compensate for the loss of the victim's honor or *enech*, which literally means "face." The expression "loss of face" is still in common use today. A person could lose face not just by being physically injured, but also by being merely insulted.

- When it came to honor prices, kings were in a class of their own for a time, but once Christianity took root, they were not quite alone at the top; bishops were given the same status as kings. Underneath kings and bishops, society was divided into three main groups: nobles, farmers, and the learned classes. Slaves were at the bottom, and they had no honor price, per se; compensation for slaves was treated simply as a property matter.

- Nobles varied in importance based on how wealthy they were—meaning how many cows they had—and also based on how many clients they had. Clients were people that received from the nobles benefits such as land, cattle, legal help, and protection. In return, nobles received benefits from their clients like labor service, dairy products, grain, malt, and meat.

- The learned classes were men were called the *filí*. There were two major kinds of *filí*: the poets (discussed in a previous lecture) and the lawyers. They had probably originally included the druids, but after the conversion to Christianity, the druids dropped out of the equation.

Law

- Irish law was referred to by the English as "brehon" law, from the Irish word *brithem*, which means "judge" or "jurist." Brehon law was one of the distinctively Irish institutions that the English tried hard to eradicate.

- Irish law looks different from, for example, the English common law, because it is mostly lists of legal rules, not records of case law. We know a lot about what the lawyers thought should happen, but not a lot about what did happen, with some exceptions. To see law in action, scholars usually have to look at what happens in stories, and law comes up enough in the stories to reinforce the importance of law to this society.

- Unlike the Anglo-Saxon kings, early Irish kings were not lawgivers, though that changed a bit with the arrival of Christianity. On the other hand, the concept of the king's justice was crucial; if the king was just, the land would produce abundant crops, but if the king was seen to be unjust, the land would wither. To act justly, kings usually enlisted the aid of judges.

- The Irish institution known as distraint caused a culture clash with the later English conquerors. Distraint was a recognized legal method of coercing someone into complying with the law. It involved depriving someone of the ability to make use of their assets, usually cattle. If someone owed compensation and refused to pay, the aggrieved party could essentially go and take the equivalent payment in actual cattle. Some of the cattle raiding endemic in Ireland was probably part of distraint.

- Another way one could obtain redress was to shame the offender into compliance by publicly fasting on their doorstep. This made a very public show of refusing this person's hospitality, which was a rebuke to their honor.

The Status of Women

- The status of women in Irish society is a huge topic, and it's very controversial among scholars. Some want to see the Celtic lands as a kind of paradise where women had greater rights than in other ancient societies. Scholars who want to argue this point to a couple of kinds of evidence.

- For instance, they note that women could initiate divorce themselves, which was not true in some other cultures. Additionally, we see occasional references to women practitioners of the learned classes: women poets, doctors, and even a satirist. It is also true that despite the fact that the normal rules of Irish property precluded the ownership of family property by women, there were clearly many instances in which women did own property.

- One of the figures most often cited when discussing the status of women in Ireland is Queen Medb of Connacht, the great antagonist of the Ulstermen in the *Táin*. The great cattle raid in that story is touched off when Medb becomes jealous of a great bull owned by her husband Ailill and wants to steal another bull to demonstrate her superiority.

- Medb casts doubt on Ailill's masculine prowess, and she offers her sexual favors to pretty much anyone who will help her get what she wants. Some scholars who have looked at Medb have assumed that any society who created a character like her must have regarded women as powerful, perhaps even as the equals of men.

- Women were very powerful in Irish folklore, and they were intimately associated with death. A battle goddess, the Morrigan, often signaled the death of a hero. The appearance of any *bean sidh*, or "fairy woman," could be the sign of impending death or misfortune, and women had the special responsibility of keening for the dead, that is, wailing in mournful tones.

- However, there is a lot of evidence for the subordinate status of women. We have lots of evidence for polygamy, at least among high-status individuals, and plenty of evidence for the sexual exploitation of women. The slave girls who notionally served as a unit of value were clearly available to their masters for that purpose. St. Patrick even refers obliquely to the mortification of female Christian converts who were forced to engage in such acts with their masters.

- It is true that women could sometimes dissolve unhappy unions, but they would then return to the legal guardianship of their male relatives. All of this evidence points not to a utopia for women but instead a complicated picture in which some women managed to carve out niches for themselves within an otherwise male-dominated society.

Suggested Reading

Binchy, "Secular Institutions."

Bitel, *Land of Women*.

Ellis, *Women in Celtic Society and Literature*.

Kelly, *A Guide to Early Irish Law*.

Ó Corráin, *Ireland before the Normans*, chapter 2.

Questions to Consider

1. What was the role of the family in Celtic society?

2. What are the difficulties in understanding the status of women in Celtic society?

Lecture

16

The Irish Sea World: Celts and Vikings

This lecture focuses on the complicated but fascinating interactions between the Celtic-speaking peoples and their neighbors all around the Irish Sea. It primarily discusses relations between the Celtic world and the Norse world, that is to say, the Vikings. We'll see that the impact of the Vikings on the various Celtic-speaking areas differed considerably. Some areas were substantially transformed by their encounter with the Vikings; other areas were barely affected at all. The lecture concentrates on the two areas where the Vikings had the most lasting effects: Ireland and Scotland.

Vikings

- The name Viking is not technically an ethnic name. It's more of a description of an occupation; to go "a-viking" meant to go out raiding. Most of the people who we call Vikings would have just called themselves Norsemen or Danes or something similar. But the name Viking has now become traditional.

- Vikings appeared on the scene in the late 8th century when small groups of raiders began attacking coastal settlements in the northern parts of the islands of Britain and Ireland. The most famous such raid took place in 793 in Lindisfarne off the east coast of the Anglian kingdom of Northumbria.

- Of all the parts of Britain and Ireland that suffered from Viking raids, the English-speaking areas were hit the worst. Ultimately, all of the major Anglo-Saxon kingdoms were knocked off by the Vikings except for one, the kingdom of Wessex in the southwest. Being the last kingdom standing, it was Wessex that benefited when the Anglo-Saxons were ultimately able to drive the Vikings out.

- The Vikings had comparatively little impact in Wales. This was because Wales was a relatively poor place at this time; there were fewer monasteries than there were elsewhere in Britain, and those monasteries contained fewer treasures. Instead, the Vikings concentrated their efforts in northern Britain and in Ireland.

Viking Activities

- Irish monasteries were raided repeatedly in some cases. It is now impossible to tell whether this was by the same band of marauders or by different ones. For example, the great monastery of Iona, which is now in Scotland but was then part of the Irish world, was raided three times in a single decade around the year 800.

- By the middle of the 9th century, Vikings were beginning to settle along the Irish coast. They created the nucleus of many of the most important towns in Ireland, including Limerick, Cork, Waterford, Wexford, and the future Irish capital, Dublin. Ireland owes its first major effort at urbanization to Scandinavian raiders.

- These settlers added to the economic strength and cultural diversity of Ireland. For example, the Vikings brought a huge infusion of cash in the form of silver, much of which had been earned in trade or plunder from the Islamic world. The Vikings also brought their sophisticated shipbuilding techniques and advanced metalworking skills to Ireland, and native craftsmen quickly adopted these techniques.

- One of the areas where the Vikings clearly excelled was in warfare, and the Irish were far from opposed to borrowing from their enemies. Perhaps the most important thing they borrowed from the Vikings was the battle-ax, a fearsome weapon.

- Assimilation was taking place in personal relationships as well. There seem to have been numerous intermarriages. For example, a mid-10th-century king of Dublin and York named Olaf Sigtryggsson married two different Irish princesses, and such marriages took place at all social levels. Those probably aided in the slow Christianization of the Viking settlements.

- The Irish saw that a group of people was appearing—the children of these interethnic unions—who were neither exclusively Irish nor exclusively Scandinavian. They came up with a word to describe these people. They called them the *Gall-Gaedhil*, which means "the foreigner-Irish." They were often bilingual in Irish and Norse, and they could function comfortably in the whole northern world that encompassed northern Ireland, Scotland, and Scandinavia.

Irish Relations

- Irish kings regarded the newcomers who had put down roots along their coastline as just one more element in a complicated local power struggle. These kings decided how to react to the Vikings on a case-by-case basis. They fought against some groups of Vikings and allied with others in an effort to improve their position against other Irish kings.

- The most important king to do so was Brian Boru, a southern Irish king who allied with Vikings to help defeat his Irish rivals. At the great Battle of Clontarf in 1014, just north of the Viking city of Dublin, Brian Boru and his Viking allies defeated another Irish king and his Viking allies.

- Ironically, this battle was later reimagined as a clash between the Irish and the Vikings, and a legend was born that stubbornly persists to this day: the notion that Brian Boru drove the Vikings out of Ireland. The real story is more interesting. The Vikings and the Irish coexisted, surely not without tension, but with advantages to both sides.

- Up until this time, Ireland had enjoyed a more or less stable system where both the northern half and the southern half of Ireland were each dominated by one major dynasty. This system began to break down in the early 10th century. One of the results of this upheaval was the rise of a new dynasty in Munster, in the southwest, that would end up replacing the dominant power there.

- This dynasty was under Brian Boru. He established his headquarters at Kincora in what is now County Clare, but he aspired to more. He started out basically confined to the south, but then he increasingly was able to move out of his own region and travel through the whole island of Ireland at will.

Brian Boru's Operations

- Brian Boru was able to take advantage of divisions within the other Irish kingdoms. He also proved to be very adept at using the Norse settlements. He forged helpful alliances with the Norse of Limerick, which was not far from Kincora, as well as Waterford and Cork, and even occasionally with Dublin. His Norse allies often held the balance of power in his favor.

- Brian Boru knew that having the church on his side would be a big help, so he made a very large donation to St. Patrick's Church at Armagh, and he installed many of his own family members at the head of important churches in Munster. He thus had the major secular and religious powers in Ireland on his side.

- However, in the year 1012, cracks began to appear in Brian Boru's dominance. The northern half of Ireland had never been as securely under his control as the south, and in that year, some northern leaders took the field against him. His ally, the king of Meath, who was still dominant in the east, fell out with the Dublin Norse. By the following year, Brian Boru was forced to blockade Dublin in support.

- The siege lasted over the winter. The Norse in Dublin knew that the attack would be renewed in the spring, so they called in their allies from the Isles (the islands around Britain, including the Orkneys and the Isle of Man). The men of Leinster, who had been chafing under Brian's overlordship for almost two decades, also got ready to move.

- Brian Boru called on his supposed allies in the north and the west, but they failed to turn out. To make matters worse, right before the imminent battle, Brian quarreled with the king of Meath, so he was relatively isolated except for a contingent of supporters from the Norse community in Limerick. Thus he went into battle at Clontarf on Good Friday, April 23, 1014.

Brian Boru

- The battle lasted all day. Eventually, Brian Boru's side routed the Leinstermen and the Dublin Norse. However, Brian Boru, who was too old and infirm to fight himself, was killed in his tent by Norsemen who were retreating in panic. The king of Leinster was also killed, though the king of the Dublin Norse managed to preserve himself by staying out of the battle completely.

- By itself it did not end the Viking presence in Ireland. The Norse communities persisted for centuries thereafter, and the end of active raiding had much less to do with Clontarf than with the conversion of Scandinavians back home to Christianity. After about 1000, the Vikings stopped raiding and mostly stayed home.

- For two centuries after the Battle of Clontarf, the Norse settlements maintained their distinctive identity, and the city of Dublin. However, the Dublin Norse were less and less able to maintain their independence and more and more likely to fall under the overlordship of one or another of the Irish provincial kings.

- When the English invaded in the 1160s and 1170s, they seized control of the Viking towns, and the new English settlers swamped the Norse element there. Still, the legacy of the Vikings in Ireland survives in the Irish cities and, as DNA testing is now showing, in the Irish people.

Scotland

- In Scotland, the Norse maintained a separate identity for far longer than they did in Ireland. The Vikings settled more extensively in parts of western and northern mainland Scotland and in the islands around Scotland. There was no English conquest of Scotland to erase their cultural presence. Thus, Scotland was much more diverse, both ethnically and linguistically, than Ireland was.

- The northern islands of Scotland, the Orkneys and Shetlands, were culturally Norse rather than Gaelic. In fact, a local variant of the Norse language, known as Norn, was spoken in those islands down to the 18th century.

- The height of the Scandinavian advance probably occurred in the middle of the 11th century with the career of the formidable Thorfinn Sigurdsson. He was able to extend Scandinavian rule onto the mainland of Scotland in the far north, and that is still the part of the mainland with the highest concentration of Norse place names, such as Sunderland, Wick, and Dingwall.

- Vikings also settled in western isles of Scotland and the Isle of Man. They created a multiethnic, multilingual territory called the Kingdom of the Isles. The later lords of the isles, who were largely autonomous, were not subdued by the Scottish crown until the end of the 15th century. Many of the clans of the western isles, including Clan MacLeod, trace their ancestry back to Norse rulers.

The Isle of Man

- The Isle of Man perfectly exemplifies the cultural fluidity of the Irish Sea region. It is right in the middle of the Irish Sea roughly equidistant from Ireland, northern England, and southern Scotland.

- The Isle of Man was a melting pot where all of the diverse influences in what historians now like to call the Irish Sea World came together. The earliest inhabitants of the Isle of Man that we know of were probably Brythonic speakers, that is, they spoke the P-Celtic language of Britain.

- At some point in the 6th century, the isle was probably occupied by people from the north of Ireland, and there may even have been a brief interlude in the 7th century when the English-speaking people of the kingdom of Northumbria seized control of the island. Thereafter, though, the main contest was between Irish and Scandinavian influence.

- In the 10th and 11th centuries, the island was ruled first by the Viking kings of Dublin and then by the Viking earls of Orkney, but the population was primarily Gaelic in culture and language. During this period, the language of Man became more distinct from Irish until it developed into the Goidelic, or Q-Celtic, language we know today as Manx.

- A watershed moment for the Isle of Man came in 1079, when the Crovan dynasty established itself on the island. Although the Crovan kings were nominally subject to the kings of Norway, it was not until the 13th century that the Norse kings were powerful enough to try to assert their dominance.

- By that point, the increasingly powerful kingdom of Scotland was interested in cracking down on Norse influence on its western periphery. In the 1260s, Scotland and Norway fought a war, partly over control of the Isle of Man, and Scotland emerged victorious.

- However, the victory was short-lived. The English and the Scots traded control of the isle over the next century or so. The Scottish king David II, who was captured by the English in 1346 at the Battle of Neville's Cross, was forced to bargain away the Isle of Man when he couldn't pay his ransom.

- With a few hiccups along the way, England has ruled the isle ever since, but it has a strange constitutional position. The Isle of Man is not subject to Britain's Parliament. It is autonomous within the United Kingdom, and it coins its own money and prints its own postage stamps. The Manx language is largely extinct, though there are efforts underway to revive it.

Suggested Reading

Lucas, "Irish-Norse Relations: Time for a Reappraisal?"
———, "The Plundering and Burning of Churches in Ireland."
Ó Corráin, *Ireland before the Normans*, chapters 1, 3, and 4.
Wormald, *Scotland*, chapter 1.

Questions to Consider

1. How did the impact of the Vikings differ in Ireland and the various regions of Britain?
2. In the long run, was Ireland better off due to the Viking invasions?

Lecture

17

English Invasions of Wales and Ireland

This lecture tells the story of two efforts by the English to conquer Celtic-speaking countries: Wales and Ireland. It begins with an overview of relations between the Welsh and the English from the period after the Anglo-Saxon settlements in the 5th and 6th centuries down through the 12th century and moves on to the fallout that followed.

Setting the Scene

- After the end of Roman rule, the Anglo-Saxons advanced from east to west across Britain, but they were stopped short in the west midlands at what we know now as the boundary with Wales.

- Over the next few hundred years, the Welsh princes continually raided the English. They were raided in turn, but they sometimes allied with one English ruler against another. For example, King Oswald of Northumbria was killed in a battle against his English enemy, the pagan king of Mercia, and Mercia's Welsh allies.

- But the Welsh did not maintain this alliance with Mercia. During the 8th century, the military threat from Wales was great enough that the Mercian king Offa built a huge dike to try to prevent Welsh attacks.

- The dike helped to preserve the status quo between the Welsh and English for many centuries, partly helped by the fact that Wales was almost always divided among rival rulers, but the relationship became strained during the reign of the next-to-last Anglo-Saxon king, Edward the Confessor. In 1055, a powerful Welsh ruler named Gruffydd ap Llywelyn managed to bring all of Wales under his command by methods that were not exactly gentle. Gruffydd then struck an alliance with a disgruntled former English earl and helped him to raid the English border town of Hereford.

Offa's Dyke

- It took the English royal forces several campaigns to subdue Gruffydd, but King Edward's right-hand man, Harold Godwinson, managed to drive him into the far northwest of Wales, where he was likely killed by one of his Welsh rivals in 1064.

- Gruffydd's death had far-reaching implications. Once he passed from the scene, Wales immediately fell apart into its traditional smaller units. This meant that two years later, when Harold Godwinson was defeated by William the Conqueror at the Battle of Hastings, Wales was going to meet the new threat not with a single strong king, but with many weak ones.

- Despite this political disadvantage for the Welsh, William never fully conquered Wales, partly because he had other lands to worry about. Over the next century or so came an ebb and flow of Anglo-Norman incursions into Wales, first in the north, and then more successfully in the south, but always rolling back the next time a truly powerful Welsh ruler presented himself. This very fluid Welsh situation played a huge role in the English invasion of Ireland.

Events in Ireland

- By the middle of the 12th century, the Irish political landscape had crystallized somewhat in comparison to an earlier period, when Ireland was ruled by a large number of regional kings. By the mid-12th century, the number of important rulers in Ireland had been whittled down to four or five at a time.

- England had also started out divided among many small kingdoms, but by the 12th century, it was incomparably more unified and more powerful than Ireland. The kings of England controlled most of western France and a significant portion of Wales.

- When King Henry II took the throne in 1154, there was talk of him invading Ireland as well, but there had been a long civil war before he became king, so he decided to concentrate on repairing that damage rather than on new conquests. However, in 1155, the pope, Adrian IV, issued the bull *Laudabiliter*, which gave the English king the authority to invade Ireland for the purposes of reforming the church.

- Ireland's major rulers tended to fall into two opposing alliances. In the 1160s, these alliances consisted of the king of Ulster and the king of Leinster on one side and the king of Connacht and the king of Breifne on the other.

- In 1166, the king of Ulster was killed. This was bad news for Diarmait Mac Murchada, king of Leinster, because he was now out of allies but not out of enemies. He had one enemy in Tigernan O'Rourke, king of Breifne. O'Rourke was a close ally of Rory O'Connor, king of Connacht, the most powerful ruler in Ireland.

A Power Struggle

- Tigernan used his influence with O'Connor to force Diarmait into exile. But Diarmait was a stubborn man. He gathered allies, including the Anglo-Norman lord Richard Strongbow. Diarmait offered Strongbow his daughter Aoife in marriage and made him heir to the kingdom of Leinster if he would come to Ireland and help get Leinster back for Diarmait.

- Strongbow wasn't ready to move as fast as Diarmait wanted him to, so Diarmait enlisted some other allies, two half-brothers: Robert FitzStephen, a Norman baron with close ties also to the Welsh aristocracy, and Maurice FitzGerald.

- The invasion unfolded in a series of expeditions, first a small group of Flemish mercenaries, then the Geraldines, and finally Strongbow himself in 1170. He brought the largest contingent of soldiers yet (200 cavalry and 1,000 archers). Within two days, Waterford had fallen, and Strongbow married Diarmait's daughter, Aoife, in Waterford Cathedral. This marriage between a foreign lord and an Irish princess was a powerful symbol of what the future held for Ireland.

- The bad news for Strongbow was that King Henry II was coming to check up on him. Henry had a sudden, quite urgent need to look good in the eyes of the church because of Henry's complicity in the murder of Thomas Becket, archbishop of Canterbury, in 1170.

- In the summer of 1171, Henry heard that papal commissioners were on their way to England to issue a condemnation for Becket's murder. It seemed like a good time to get out of the area and to be seen to be doing the church's business while he was at it. Henry invoked *Laudabiliter* at last and made plans to depart for Ireland with an even larger army than Strongbow had, plus siege equipment.

- Strongbow submitted and accepted Henry's terms. Henry called a church council. Lots of reforming legislation was passed, the bishops accepted Henry as overlord of Ireland, and the pope was gratified. By September

1172, Henry was officially forgiven for Becket's murder, due in no small part to his Irish expedition.

Under Henry II

- As soon as Henry returned to his own lands, war broke out again between the English invaders and the Irish lords. Henry decided he would need to reorganize English rule in Ireland, and he decided to set up a lordship there for his youngest son, John.

- When John actually went to Ireland in 1185, he made a total mess of the expedition. The result was that Ireland remained divided among the Irish and the English in a patchwork. There were areas where the English were quite dominant, and others where they were very thin on the ground.

- John left in disgust, and he would not return to Ireland until 25 years later, in 1210. At that point, he mainly came to punish his own rebellious barons. No English king returned to Ireland after that for nearly 300 years. Thus, Henry II's scheme for an Irish kingdom with, perhaps, a resident monarch, came to naught.

- Once John withdrew, the Anglo-Norman settlers were left practically to their own devices to try to expand their holdings at the expense of the Irish. One important step the settlers took was to construct a network of castles to help them to secure their lands against Irish attacks. These castles grew up somewhat haphazardly in places where the settlers felt able to build them, and they clearly clustered along the east coast.

Politics in Ireland

- The arrival of so many armed and determined English soldiers had effectively ended any hopes that the Irish would develop a unified kingdom. Irish politics were not merely fractured; due to the various encroachments of the Anglo-Norman lords, even provincial kingships had vanished.

- The small lordships that remained among the Irish were still not territorial entities but rather networks of relationships, all of which were extremely fluid. At the top was the over-king and his family, any of whom might be in rebellion against him at any given time. Underneath were the chiefs, some of whom were descended from formerly semiautonomous minor kings, who controlled their own kinsmen and clients. These were notoriously unreliable. It was always a matter of suspense whether they would turn out when summoned.

- The Anglo-Norman lords and agents of the English crown happily inserted themselves into these fluid networks. Just as the Vikings had been absorbed into local Irish politics, these newcomers also made alliances with the Irish. The Irish did not have any scruples about using the newcomers to score points against their own Irish rivals.

- However, this system did not work as well as it had with the Vikings, who were ultimately absorbed into Irish society. The problem was that the English had a very different attitude to grants of land. They were meant to be perpetual, and once someone put castles on them, it was hard to get rid of them.

- When the Irish thought they were making a clever alliance to meet the political contingencies of the moment, they were actually letting in men who would not be so easily contained or sent packing when they were no longer useful. As a result, the Anglo-Norman lords, who had sometimes been installed with Irish backing, became often not tools of the Irish but the dominant players in local politics. They took the place of the old over-kings.

- Since the Anglo-Irish lords felt increasingly that they were on their own, they figured that if it was up to them to protect their own estates, they would use whatever methods seemed best to them. Many times, this meant adapting to local conditions and adopting Irish forms of warfare, the use of Irish law, and the use of the Irish language.

The Statutes of Kilkenny

- Another big factor that helped the native Irish inhabitants and hurt the English colonists was the Black Death. It spread throughout Europe and reached Ireland in 1348, first in the southeast and then spreading to the north and west. It was disproportionately severe in the towns, which was where the English lived. People began giving up and moving back to

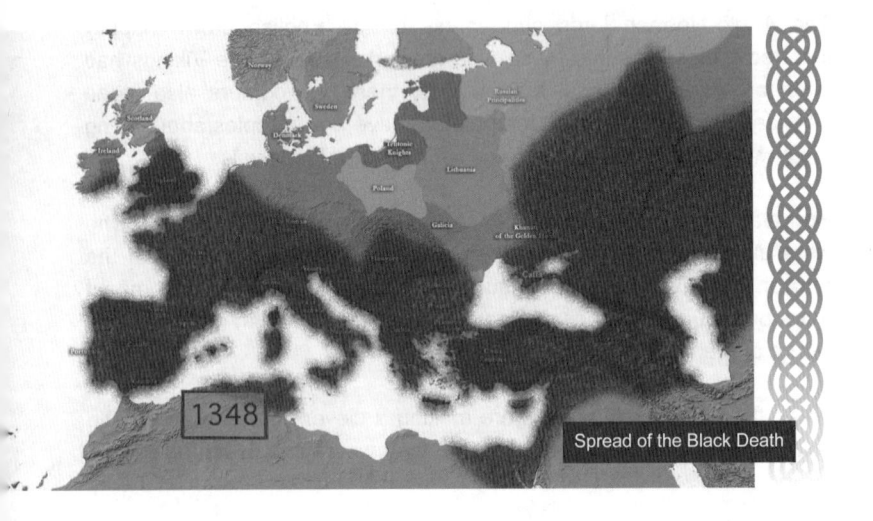

Spread of the Black Death

England. By the late 14th century, there were laws passed trying to stop English settlers from returning and also trying to force English settlers who had already moved back to England to return.

- Ireland had gone from providing revenue to being a net drain on the English treasury. In 1361, King Edward III had his son, Lionel, marry the heiress to the earldom of Ulster, and he sent him to Ireland to rule on his behalf. Lionel did his best, but he was horrified that the English settlers were acting like Irishmen. He called a parliament at Kilkenny to try to address the problem.

- This parliament produced the notorious Statutes of Kilkenny in 1366. They ordered that the Anglo-Irish, that is, people who had been settled in Ireland for generations, should not be treated any differently from Englishmen who had just arrived in the country.

- There was also a list of Irish things the English weren't allowed to do. The Anglo-Irish were ordered to speak only English among themselves; the law thus recognized the necessity of speaking Irish when dealing with Irish neighbors, but they did not want any use of Irish when it wasn't strictly necessary for such a purpose.

- Along the same lines, the Anglo-Irish were not to use Irish names or ride horses in the Irish style, that is, bareback with no stirrups. They were not supposed to get Irish haircuts: shaved on top and long in back (which looked a bit like a mullet). There was thus supposed to be a cultural wall between Irish and English that would seal the two ethnic groups off from each other.

- However, some English settlers in Ireland became so enamored of Irish culture that they not only learned the Irish language but even wrote poetry in Irish. In fact, the third earl of Desmond, Gerald FitzGerald, who was alive at the time of the Statutes, wrote quite good Irish poetry.

- The problem with the statutes was that they were put in under the assumption that changing the languages and haircuts of people would change the political realities on the ground. In fact, a lot of assimilation on the part of the Anglo-Irish was really an effort to survive in an increasingly precarious environment.

- One of the provisions of the statutes was that the Anglo-Irish should not use Irish law to settle disputes, but what was a person supposed to do if they lived in an area where that was the only law available? The statutes were thus trying to legislate about hair and saddles and other such things when the real problem was the lack of infrastructure that could support an English-style government.

- Keep in mind that however much the government wanted to make distinctions, there was no hard and fast line between English and Irish. Cultural assimilation did not always make the settlers forget who their ancestors were, but even within a single family, there were wide variations in practice.

- The Irish wanted more help from England but were often dissatisfied with the help they were sent. They were in a very ambivalent situation, and it was not going to get better until the Tudor government decided to resolve the Irish question once and for all.

Suggested Reading

Flanagan, *Irish Society, Anglo-Norman Settlers*, Angevin Kingship.
Frame, *Colonial Ireland*.
———, *English Lordship in Ireland*.
Gerald of Wales, *The Conquest of Ireland*.
———, *The History and Topography of Ireland*.
Maund, *The Welsh Kings*, chapters 1–3.

Questions to Consider:

1. What factors contributed to the (partial) conquest of Ireland?
2. To what extent did English settlers in Ireland assimilate into Irish society?

Lecture

18

Scotland from *Macbeth* to *Braveheart*

This lecture tells the story of Scotland from about the 11th century to the early 14th century. It focuses on the story of the creation of the kingdom of Scotland, and it looks at the role that ethnicity played in that process, particularly Celtic ethnicity. Along the way, the lecture introduces some of the most intriguing figures in Scottish history: Macbeth, Sir William Wallace, and Robert the Bruce.

Background on Scotland

- Before the time period the bulk of this lecture looks at, Scotland had been open to many influences over the years. There were Celtic-speaking Picts in the northeast and the Celtic-speaking Britons in the southwest. Also present were Germanic-speaking Angles in the southeast and Germanic-speaking Scandinavians in the far north and the western islands. Everywhere else were the Celtic-speaking Gaels who traced their cultural lineage to Ireland. By the 9th century, Scotland was very multiethnic and very multilingual.

- In the 9th and 10th centuries, there was an amalgamation between the areas of Pictish influence and the areas of Irish influence. They ended up creating a unitary Scottish kingdom in the heartland of what later became Scotland, from the central belt between Edinburgh and Glasgow up north into the Highlands.

- The losers in this process seem to have been the Picts, in the sense that their language and culture died out, but this does not necessarily mean that anything terrible happened to the people. They probably just adopted a Gaelic identity.

- Later written sources place this consolidation of the Picts and Scots during the reign of Kenneth MacAlpin, who supposedly reigned from 810 to 858. This newly consolidated kingdom slowly but surely absorbed the British kingdoms in the southwest and forced the English and the Scandinavians out. This process took many centuries, and it was rather messy. Not everybody in Scotland wanted there to be one powerful Scottish king, and even those who did believe in a unified kingdom often disagreed very strongly about who should rule it.

Macbeth

- Macbeth is certainly a famous figure due to Shakespeare's play, but this lecture looks at him because he is a perfect example of how Celtic sensibilities came to seem alien to later people who had been influenced by English political and cultural norms. Macbeth was a very Celtic ruler, but he was stigmatized later as a villain in order to make the Scottish ruling house look less Celtic and thus less barbaric.

- Macbeth was born around 1005 into the newly consolidated Scottish kingdom that was both facing enemies on its periphery and frequently torn by internal conflict. The main reason for the turmoil was the Scottish system of succession to the throne, which was common to other parts of the Celtic-speaking world.

- In 11th-century Scotland, the rules were quite loose. A successor needed to be related to the previous king; ideally, the successor would be his oldest son, but the most important factor was not one's exact position in the royal genealogy. It was one's competence to rule, and that was determined very much by whether one could project an image of strength to their followers.

- Macbeth was probably the grandson of King Malcolm II through his mother. His father was the ruler of Moray, an important territory in the north of Scotland. When King Malcolm died in 1034, the kingdom went to another grandson, Duncan, the son of Malcolm's daughter Bethoc. Duncan and Macbeth were probably fairly close in age.

> In the centuries after his death, Scottish writers damaged Macbeth's reputation. Shakespeare's Macbeth was nearly all created by the Scots themselves.

- Duncan ruled for six years, and then he was killed by Macbeth, but not as we see in Shakespeare's play. It's not a cold-blooded murder. Macbeth killed Duncan in battle while pursuing his own claim to the throne. Furthermore, that battle took place on Macbeth's home turf. Duncan had invaded Macbeth's territory in the north because Macbeth had become a threat to him.

- Macbeth then ruled relatively successfully for 17 years. Ultimately, though, Macbeth lost the kingdom just as he had gained it: in battle with a rival, Malcolm III, son of Duncan. Malcolm III's reign marked the beginning of a period of English influence in Scotland that profoundly shaped the creation of the Scottish kingdom and ultimately helped to dilute the Celtic elements in Scottish politics and culture.

- Malcolm had regained his throne with the help of his uncle, Earl Siward of Northumbria, indicating that Scotland and England were by no means sealed off from each other in this period. In fact, they were always interconnected, even if they were frequently at war. For many centuries, England and Scotland harbored each other's exiles.

Norman Activities

- The Norman conquest of England in 1066, led by William the Conqueror, is famous to many people. A less well-known aspect of this conquest is the fact that even after the English king, Harold Godwinson, was killed at the Battle of Hastings, there was a royal English claimant who survived.

- This claimant was named Edgar Aetheling. When King Harold died at Hastings and William began his devastating march towards London, Edgar's supporters rather quickly rushed to meet William and offer him submission. Edgar was forced to follow suit, but within a few years, Edgar's resolve stiffened, and he ended up in Scotland at the court of Malcolm III.

William the Conqueror

- King Malcolm agreed to marry one of Edgar's sisters, Margaret, and to support Edgar's bid for the English throne. It's very probable that part of the deal would have been a promise that Scotland would receive territory in northern England in return for this assistance.

- William was a formidable adversary, and Malcolm paid a heavy price for supporting Edgar. Malcolm had to acknowledge William's overlordship and expel Edgar from Scotland. Edgar duly went into exile.

- The marriage between Edgar's sister Margaret and King Malcolm was long and lasting; in fact, the two spouses were so devoted to each other that when Margaret learned of Malcolm's death in battle in 1093, she died three days later, supposedly of grief. She was renowned for her piety and was canonized in 1250 by the Catholic Church.

- Because Edgar never married, and his other sister Christina became a nun, Queen Margaret of Scotland represented the true line of the Anglo-Saxon royal house. In 1100, William the Conqueror's youngest son, who had just taken the English throne as Henry I, decided to unite the old Anglo-Saxon claim to the Norman claim by marrying the daughter of Queen Margaret and Malcolm, Princess Edith. Edith was then renamed Matilda so that the French-speaking Normans could pronounce her name.

- Matilda, the half-Scottish, half-Anglo-Saxon queen of England, invited her younger brother David to spend time at the English court, and while he was there, he became thoroughly Normanized. He absorbed some of the practices that we loosely refer to as feudalism, and he ultimately brought them back to Scotland. Due to the unexpected early deaths of all of his older brothers, he became king of Scotland in 1124 and ruled for nearly 30 years.

- David admired the Anglo-Norman knights he met at the English, so he invited many of them to Scotland and gave them lands and titles. These knights founded many of the great families of Scotland, including two families that would later produce royal Scottish dynasties: the Bruce family, who were originally from Normandy, and the Stuart family, who came from Brittany.

- Some of these families assimilated very well into the existing Gaelic-speaking aristocracy of Scotland. However, the Anglo-Norman element helped to make the French language and later the Scots language, which was closely related to English, more prestigious than Gaelic. That is one reason why Scots became the country's dominant language.

Changing Customs

- King David was a very Anglicized Gaelic king of Scotland, and this trend continued over the next century and a half. Most of the 13th century was peaceful enough until the Scottish royal family underwent a dynastic catastrophe in 1286, when King Alexander III died, leaving only a granddaughter, who promptly died as well.

- Under the old Celtic conditions of Macbeth's day, there would have been a civil war to decide which of the 13 throne-worthy men who presented themselves should become king. But the Scots had now become accustomed to following Anglo-Norman-style dynastic rules, so King Edward I of England was called in to mediate among the claimants, who argued their cases based not on competence but on genealogy.

- King Edward wasn't going to pick the most formidable candidate. He instead elected John Balliol, another scion of a northern French family, over a more popular candidate named Robert de Brus, or Robert Bruce, who was likewise of mixed Anglo-Norman and Celtic ancestry. Balliol was largely unable to stand up to King Edward's efforts to dominate Scotland, and he lost support quickly among the Scottish nobles.

- John Balliol eventually did defy Edward, but by then it was too late. In 1296, Edward marched north, defeated Balliol, and took him captive. Edward also removed the coronation stone of the Scottish kings from

Scone Abbey and installed it at Westminster Abbey as if to say Scottish sovereignty was now at an end. This brings the lecture up to the events that are rather loosely depicted in the film *Braveheart*.

Braveheart

- The hero of *Braveheart* is a real historical figure named Sir William Wallace, played by Mel Gibson, who nearly singlehandedly takes on the English oppressors of Scotland. There are problems in *Braveheart*, but it is true that Wallace did make life very difficult for the English in Scotland for nearly a decade. He did defeat them at Stirling Bridge in 1297, and he was named Guardian of Scotland. Finally, though, he was captured in 1305 and executed in a very gruesome fashion.

Sir William Wallace

- At the same time, though, another Robert Bruce, the grandson of the unsuccessful claimant from back in the early 1290s, took over the leadership of the Scottish resistance to English rule after murdering yet another claimant to the throne in 1306. He went on to defeat the English at the Battle of Bannockburn in 1314. Scotland maintained its independence from England for almost three more centuries.

- Scotland only became part of Britain in 1603 by a dynastic accident, when Queen Elizabeth I died without heirs and left the kingdom to her cousin, James VI of Scotland, who became James I of England.

Robert Bruce's Activities

- During his day, Bruce knew he was locked in a life-and-death struggle to maintain Scottish independence, and he reached out for allies wherever he could find them. There is some evidence that he was trying, from early on in his reign, to create an alliance with Ireland and Wales. He wrote a letter to the Irish kings in 1306 in which he specifically referred to the common ancestry of the Irish and the Scots.

- In 1315, the year after his big victory at the Battle of Bannockburn, Bruce tried to bring such an alliance about. He clearly saw a Scottish invasion of Ireland as a way to cut off the supply of Irish troops and taxes to the English army.

- Around the time of Bannockburn, Robert Bruce was approached by Donal O'Neill, an Irish ruler who wanted help against the earl of Ulster, Robert's former father-in-law. The O'Neills were the most illustrious native family in Ireland. In response to O'Neill's plea, Robert Bruce sent his brother, Edward, to Ireland. In May of 1315, Edward landed in Ulster, and many Irish leaders flocked to join him. He set up his base in Ulster, and he also raided the midlands and the south.

- Edward also participated in a ritual of royal inauguration. He was claiming to be king of Ireland, which many people acknowledged. Edward had some successes. He did beat the earl of Ulster in the field. He captured the imposing castle of Carrickfergus, the great fortress of the earls of Ulster. But he could not capture Dublin, so he still could not operate consistently outside of his initial power base in Ulster.

- In 1317, Robert Bruce decided to come in person to try to jump-start the invasion. Together, the brothers moved south on Dublin, but the city resisted. They bypassed Dublin and moved south into Munster, where they went up against an Anglo-Irish army, which also included one faction of the famous O'Brien family. The Bruces were forced to retreat back to Ulster. Robert was needed back in Scotland, so he went home. For a year and a half, Edward sat in Ulster, unable to do much of anything.

- During this period of stalemate in 1317, Donal O'Neill drafted a document called the *Remonstrance of the Irish Princes*. It was sent by the Irish princes to Pope John XXII. The remonstrance came about because the Irish lords had a public relations problem. Officially, they were rebels. From the perspective of the rest of Europe, including the church, the Irish princes were supposed to be subjects of the king of England.

- However, they had switched allegiance and accepted Edward Bruce. How could they justify defying the terms of the papal bull *Laudabiliter*, which had authorized the English invasion of Ireland back in the 12th century? The remonstrance tries to explain, and in effect, it tries to have it both ways. First, it denies that *Laudabiliter* is valid. This was a risky strategy because it's not easy to get a pope to overturn something his predecessor did.

- The remonstrance also draws heavily on *The Book of Invasions*, the amalgam of origin myths about the Irish that dates back in some form at least to the 8th century. The Irish princes cite their descent from the Milesians of Spain and thus deny that England has any authority over them.

Robert Bruce

- The pope ignored the remonstrance, and the rebel princes were later excommunicated. Finally, in the fall of 1318, fed up with this situation, Edward Bruce decided on a last big action. He moved south again and came to battle at Faughart, near Dundalk on the coast, but he was defeated and died in the battle. That was the end of the Bruce invasion.

- It failed for many reasons, but one of the most important was the fact that there was no real pan-Celtic alliance; there wasn't even a pan-Irish alliance. Edward Bruce had a powerful ally in Donal O'Neill, but O'Neill could not speak for the lords of the rest of Ireland. They saw no reason automatically to back this invader. Wherever there was a faction fight, the factions would split into pro-Bruce and anti-Bruce parties, and that division doomed the invasion.

Fallout

- The Bruce invasion of Ireland probably had a direct impact on one of the most important documents in Scottish history, the famous *Declaration of Arbroath*, which was written in 1320, only three years after the *Remonstrance of the Irish Princes*. It, too, was directed at the pope to explain the fact that the Scots were supporting their king, Robert Bruce, who had been excommunicated for murdering his rival for the throne back in 1306.

- The declaration starts by explaining the proud heritage of the Scots back to Spain, and before that to the Mediterranean and to Scythia. All of this is borrowed directly from the Irish *Book of Invasions*, so it's highly likely that the Irish and Scottish intellectuals had been talking to each other about the best way to project an image of independence to the pope. The *Declaration of Arbroath* was more successful than the *Remonstrance of the Irish Princes*, since Pope John XXII did eventually lift Robert Bruce's excommunication.

- In the wake of the wars of independence against England, there was an explosion of Scottish historical writing. In around 1375, a long poem was written in Scots to commemorate the achievements of Robert Bruce. About 100 years later, another poem was written by someone calling himself Blind Harry about the deeds of William Wallace. This is a far less factual account than the Bruce poem, and it served as the basis for the novel that eventually became the film *Braveheart*.

Suggested Reading

Barrow, *Kingship and Unity*.

Cowan, *The Wallace Book*.

Duffy, *Robert the Bruce's Irish Wars*.

Duncan, *Scotland: The Making of the Kingdom*, chapters 5–22.

Wormald, *Scotland*, chapters 1–3.

Questions to Consider:

1. How did the ethnic and linguistic map of Scotland change over time?

2. What was the impact of the Scottish relationship with England on the development of the Scottish kingdom?

Lecture

19

Politics and Literature in Wales

This lecture tells the story of Wales from the 11th century down to about the 15th century. It discusses the tangled politics within Wales itself and the complicated relationship between Wales and England that culminated in the conquest of Wales. The lecture also touches on fascinating literature of medieval Wales.

Welsh Society

- Wales, like Ireland, was very culturally unified, but it was politically divided, partly due to its geography. The terrain is quite mountainous, and the topography is challenging enough to make it easy for authority to be fragmented into small units, perhaps as small in some cases as a single valley.

- Nevertheless, there were several large centers of power, or petty kingdoms, but the ability of these kings or lords to control their followers was very tenuous. Persistent succession struggles continually worked against the creation of political stability.

- Throughout the Middle Ages, Wales was divided along geographic lines roughly into thirds. In the south, there were a series of small kingdoms, ranging from Dyfed in the southwest to Gwent in the southeast. In central Wales, the dominant power was the kingdom of Powys. The most important lordship, however, was arguably Gwynedd in the northwest, where several generations of rulers were able to exert a loose overlordship over many of the other Welsh princes.

- The most important geographic fact in Welsh history has been the relationship with its larger and richer neighbor to the east. The history of relations between England and Wales is long and complicated. It goes back to the period of the Germanic settlements, when the area of Celtic speech slowly receded westward across the country.

- A more or less stable situation developed whereby Celtic-speaking rulers were confined to the area we now know as Wales, but there was still considerable cross-border raiding between Wales and the various English kingdoms. It was to defend against such raids that King Offa of the English kingdom of Mercia built his famous dike in the 8th century, large sections of which can still be seen today.

- In the subsequent few centuries, there were occasional serious incidents when Welsh rulers would cause trouble on the English side of the border or vice versa, but these raids were usually rather ephemeral. The dynamic changed considerably with the Norman conquest of England in 1066. Under the early Norman kings, English settlers made inroads in Wales intending not just to seize plunder or teach the natives a lesson, but rather to settle permanently.

- The Normans had some lasting successes, especially in the south, where they created a colony in what is now Pembrokeshire. However, the Normans had never really conquered the whole place. Conversely, because the Welsh fought with each other as much as they did with the English, they had great difficulty in unifying sufficiently to see off the English threat for good.

Llywelyn the Great

- Periodically, Wales did produce leaders who made a run at establishing hegemony over the whole country. The most important came from Gwynedd, and this lecture will discuss two of them; both were named Llywelyn.

- The first was Llywelyn ap Iorwerth. He was also known as Llywelyn the Great. He earned that nickname by extending his overlordship over much of Wales and by dealing with the English on virtually an equal footing. One of the clearest signs of Llywelyn's authority was the fact that he made a peace treaty with King John of England in 1200, and he even married John's illegitimate daughter, Joan.

- Llywelyn ap Iorwerth tried to at least partly assimilate Wales to English norms. The relationship between Llywelyn ap Iorwerth and King John of England did not work out well, however. Llywelyn ap Iorwerth seems to have allied himself with the English noble family of de Braose, which held lands along the Welsh border.

- When the de Braoses fell out with King John, Llywelyn ap Iorwerth was drawn into the dispute. King John's supporter, the earl of Chester, attacked Gwynedd. In 1211, King John invaded Gwynedd personally. John was supported by most of the other princes of Wales, who were willing to ally with John in order to put Llywelyn in his place and preserve their own autonomy.

Llywelyn the Great

- Though he was able to capture hostages—and execute some of them—John's Welsh efforts were abandoned owing to resistance from Llywelyn ap Iorwerth and allies he gathered. A few years later, the text of the Magna Carta treaty would specifically call on John to release the remaining Welsh hostages, including one of Llywelyn ap Iorwerth's illegitimate sons. Llywelyn ap Iorwerth went on to rule Gwynedd and to dominate Wales until his death in 1240.

Llywellyn ap Gruffydd

- The second Llywelyn this lecture discusses is Llywelyn the Great's grandson, Llywelyn ap Gruffydd. He was the son of Llywelyn the Great's illegitimate son Gruffydd, a hostage who was released under the terms of the Magna Carta.

- Llywelyn the Great had passed over Gruffydd in the succession in favor of his legitimate son Dafydd, whose mother was Princess Joan. After the death of their father, the two half-brothers fought each other for the rulership of Gwynedd. The English king Henry III used this internecine dispute to his advantage to keep the Welsh at each other's throats. By 1246, Llywelyn ap Gruffydd was the last man standing.

- The final conquest of Wales came about when Llywelyn ap Gruffydd clashed with the son and successor of King Henry III, Edward I, over the feudal homage that Llywelyn ap Gruffydd supposedly owed to the English king under the terms of the Treaty of Montgomery, signed in 1267.

- Throughout the 1270s, there were repeated clashes between Edward and Llywellyn. The English king made use of Llywellyn ap Gruffydd's resentful and treacherous younger brother Dafydd, who had actually plotted to assassinate Llywellyn ap Gruffydd as a means of fomenting discontent in Gwynedd.

- The end came in 1282, and it was precipitated by Dafydd. Many of the Welsh lords who were now effectively under English lordship thought better of their support for English rule once it became clear that Edward would be a harsh overlord, and Dafydd himself precipitated a rebellion against the English. Llywellyn ap Gruffydd felt obliged to support his brother for some reason, and he was forced into a war that he was ill prepared to fight. In December 1282, Llywellyn was killed in battle, and his head was displayed in London for the next 15 years.

- After Llywellyn's death, King Edward made it his business to conquer all of Wales once and for all. He made sure of his conquest by building a series of impressive castles, many of which still stand today. The country was suppressed remarkably quickly. There were a few uprisings, but nothing major until the revolt of Owain Glyndwr in 1400, made famous in Shakespeare's play *Henry IV, Part I*.

- Owain was a substantial figure. He was descended from the native princes of Powys in central Wales, and he entered into a major conspiracy with two English rebel lords, with the idea that the three men would divide the island of Britain three ways. Owain's two English confederates were defeated at the Battle of Shrewsbury in 1403, but Owain managed to hang on against the English until 1409, when he was forced into hiding. He was last spotted in 1412.

Welsh Literature

- The lecture now turns to medieval Welsh literature. The corpus of medieval Welsh literature is not as extensive as the Irish one, but it has arguably been far more influential on European literature as a whole.

- Much of what we have is preserved in two manuscripts. One is the *White Book of Rydderch*, so called because it is bound in white leather, which was written in southwest Wales in about 1350. The other is the *Red Book of Hergest*, this one bound in red leather, which was written after 1382 along the border with England.

- The oldest Welsh literary texts we have are poems from the early Middle Ages. They include some beautiful laments for the loss of love and youth, as well as the epic poem *Gododdin*. Much of what was produced from the 11th century onward consists of praise poetry for the Welsh princes.

- The most influential works of Welsh medieval literature, however, are the four anonymous prose tales known collectively as the *Mabinogi* as well as the tales that relate to King Arthur (which will be discussed in a later lecture). The *Mabinogi* can be a puzzling work.

- The four tales are often referred to as the four branches. They are interrelated, with some characters that occur in more than one of the stories, but the relationship between them doesn't seem especially close.

- In the first branch, which is called "Pwyll, Prince of Dyfed," the title character, Pwyll, does a service for the lord of the underworld, Arawn. He is rewarded with a mysterious supernatural bride named Rhiannon, who rides a horse that can never be caught up with. Rhiannon and Pwyll have many adventures before they can finally marry, but Rhiannon eventually bears a son, Pryderi. The core of the story is the disappearance of the infant Pryderi, for which Rhiannon is initially blamed. However, Pryderi is eventually restored to his rightful place and succeeds Pwyll in ruling Dyfed.

- In the second branch, which is called "Branwen, Daughter of Llyr," we have completely new characters. Branwen is the sister of Brân the Blessed, king of Britain. The king of Ireland, Matholwch, asks for her hand in marriage, which Brân grants, but because Branwen's half-brother Efnisien is not consulted on the matter, he angrily mutilates the horses of the Irish delegation, and a lasting resentment is created.

- Once Branwen is back in Ireland, she produces a son, Gwern, but she is badly treated at the Irish court, and the king forces her to work in the kitchens. She trains a starling to bring word of her predicament back to King Brân, who invades Ireland on her behalf.

- Brân is a giant. He is so large that he can wade across the Irish Sea. Once he arrives, Branwen makes peace between her husband and her brother, but war breaks out again due to Efnisien, who seizes his nephew Gwern and throws him on the fire. The two sides proceed to slaughter each other (though the action is prolonged by the fact that the Irish possess a magic cauldron that can bring the dead back to life).

- Brân is finally killed as well, and his head is cut off, though it continues to talk. The head is then buried in London at the site of the later Tower of London where it will supposedly ward off invasion. Branwen also returns to Britain only to die of grief. The other two branches contain the same marvelous mixture of supernatural elements and human drama.

- A Welsh literary figure who lived a bit later than the authors of the *Mabinogi*, during the period after the English conquest, was the great poet Dafydd ap Gwilym. Dafydd lived in the middle of the 14th century, though we are unsure of the exact dates. He wrote with great wit and verve about both love and nature. Here is an excerpt from "The Girls of Llanbadarn:

> I am twisted with passion—plague on all the girls of the parish! since I suffered from trysts which went amiss, and could never win a single one of them, neither gentle hopeful maid, nor little lass, nor hag, nor wife.

- The reader gets to know the poet and his personal frustrations and delights. Despite the political difficulties the Welsh experienced, they were able to take refuge in a remarkable literary tradition that laid the foundations for what is arguably the strongest surviving Celtic language today.

Dafydd ap Gwilym

Suggested Reading

Davies, *A History of Wales*, chapters 4–5.

Dillon and Chadwick, *The Celtic Realms*, chapter 11.

Ford, ed. and trans., *The Mabinogi and Other Medieval Welsh Tales*.

Loomis, ed. and trans., *Dafydd ap Gwilym*.

Maund, *The Welsh Kings*, chapters 3–7.

Rees and Rees, *Celtic Heritage*.

Questions to Consider

1. How did Welsh political structures contribute to the English conquest of Wales?

2. What makes the stories in the Mabinogi appealing to modern readers, and what makes them challenging?

Lecture

20

The Tudor Conquest of Ireland

This lecture tells the story of the final clash between the English and the Irish that led to the Tudor conquest of Ireland. Along the way, we will look particularly at the question of how Irish identity played a role in English policy in Ireland. The lecture uses the example of the experience of one of the most important families in Irish history, the O'Neills, who had to figure out repeatedly where they stood on the spectrum between Irish and English identity. We'll also look at the English policy of plantation, which was a concerted effort to wipe out Irish culture (if not the Irish themselves) and turn Ireland into another England.

Background

- This lecture's conflict has deep roots in the Middle Ages. The English had never completely conquered Ireland, and as a result, there was an uneasy coexistence on the island between the Irish and the English settlers. This situation was inherently unstable, and from the late 15th century through the 16th century, the English government tried a number of expedients in an effort to solve the so-called Irish problem.

- The question of how to rule Ireland was suddenly crucially important in the 1530s, when Henry VIII broke with the Catholic Church. All of a sudden, England was on the wrong side of the major Catholic powers in Europe, particularly Spain, which was especially aggrieved that the Reformation in England had been touched off by Henry's rejection of his Spanish bride, Catherine of Aragon. Ireland now represented a security threat for England because it was a perfect back door for the Spanish to use in a potential invasion of England.

Catherine of Aragon

194 | Lecture 20 ● The Tudor Conquest of Ireland

- From the 1530s on, in addition to military action when required, the English government pursued two other main avenues toward pacification of Ireland. The first was Anglicization, an effort to convert the Irish to adopting English behaviors and customs. The second approach was Protestantization, an attempt to bring the Irish to the new English state religion.

Surrender and Regrant

- One of the most interesting experiments in this effort to convert the Irish to both Protestantism and Englishness came during the reign of Henry VIII. This was the policy that later historians have called surrender and regrant. The main idea was to try to turn the leaders of the Irish community into good English lords, and that would make them loyal; then the lower social ranks in Ireland would naturally follow along.

- An Irish lord would acknowledge the king's authority in Ireland and receive in exchange a grant of the territory he already held. Where previously the English government might not have recognized the Irish lord's right to the land, now he would be treated as English. He would be equal in law to an English nobleman. In return, he would be expected to adopt English customs and learn English.

- Probably the two most impressive catches were the two most important Irish chiefs from Ulster, Manus O'Donnell and Conn O'Neill. After making significant concessions, the latter was made the first earl of Tyrone. This was a huge propaganda success for the English.

- Surrender and regrant had a troubled legacy. It did succeed in integrating many Irish lords into the English system. But there was also some pushback from people who felt that surrender and regrant was a betrayal of Irish culture. Prominent among these detractors were the Irish bards.

Plantation

- When it became clear early on that surrender and regrant was not going to put an end to Irish rebellions, the English turned to another policy with far-reaching consequences in Irish history: plantation. The idea was to bring in English people and turn an area into a de facto island of Englishness.

- Plantation was started in the 1540s and 1550s in response to a revolt in the Irish midlands, and then extended to the southwest in the 1580s. The legal basis for plantation was the continued rebellion of the natives against royal authority. The English issued bills of attainder against the rebels.

- A bill of attainder is a law passed against a named individual, in this case, specific Irish rebels. Under these bills, their lands were confiscated. Parliament passed laws against the specific Irish rebels whose land they wanted to confiscate. Once the land had been confiscated, it had to be Anglicized.

- The highly Anglicizing policy of plantation got its start under a Catholic monarch of England, namely, Mary Tudor. For Mary, the status of the Irish as Catholics did not wipe out the problem of their being Irish. But because Mary died soon after plantation got underway, and the religious policy of the English government shifted with it, plantation quickly got associated in people's minds with Protestantism. This made those who didn't like plantation turn against Protestantism, and it made those who didn't like Protestantism resist plantation.

Balancing Demands

- In 1559, Conn O'Neill, the earl of Tyrone, died, leaving two sons as claimants to the earldom, Matthew (the elder and therefore the official English-sponsored claimant) and Shane (the younger, but the most prominent of the claimants under the Irish system). For the English, it would have been simplest to recognize Shane O'Neill as earl, because Shane was the strongest claimant and a very able diplomat and military leader.

- However, there were reasons not to recognize him. Shane had close ties to the Scots, who were not friendly towards the English at this point, and he was arming local peasants in an apparent effort to prepare for rebellion. In June 1561, with the queen's patience running out, Shane was invited to London for negotiations.

- Peace seemed to be at hand, but during Shane's visit to London, Shane's rival, Matthew O'Neill, was assassinated. His killers threw their support behind a different O'Neill claimant named Turlough Luineach.

- This led Shane to return to Ireland to try to fight for his rights among his own kin, and because he had broken the peace with the English government, he was now at war with England. It took nearly five years to suppress the rebellion, and it only ended when Shane was forced to seek help from a local Ulster lord with Scottish connections named Alexander Óg MacDonnell. Shane was received with signs of friendship and then killed during a banquet, no doubt as part of a conspiracy with the English.

Major Revolts

- The O'Neills were not finished yet. The lecture now turns to the last major revolts in Ireland during the reign of Elizabeth I. The Nine Years' War, which began in 1593, dwarfed any previous rebellion in scope and size. It posed the most serious threat to English rule in Ireland, mainly because of the fear of Spanish intervention in Ireland. English and Irish forces in this revolt were well balanced.

- The key figure in this revolt was a man named Hugh O'Neill. Hugh O'Neill was the second son of Matthew O'Neill, the English-sanctioned heir to the first earl of Tyrone, Conn O'Neill. Hugh had become the official English claimant to the earldom when he was only 12 years old. His childhood shows us how these Irish noblemen were increasingly operating in two worlds, Irish and English.

- When Hugh became the heir, he was brought to the Pale, the area around Dublin that was culturally English, and then raised partly in England, so he was completely bilingual. He came back to Ireland in 1567 and served in Queen Elizabeth's army against the Irish rebels in southern Ireland, and he even fought with an English contingent that was aiding the Protestant rebels against Spanish rule in the Netherlands.

- Hugh's goal was to combine both the English title (earl of Tyrone) and the Irish chieftaincy (head of the O'Neills) in one person: himself. The trouble was that the claimant to the chieftaincy who was around at the time of Shane's revolt, Turlough Luinneach O'Neill, still had widespread support. It took the better part of three decades for Hugh to work both systems and get both the English to recognize him as earl of Tyrone and the Irish to recognize him as chieftain.

- All of this careful work was undone by the Nine Years' War. It was started in 1593 by an alliance of other northern lords in combination with some prominent Catholic clerics. One of these clerics, Archbishop James O'Hely of Tuam, went to seek aid from Spain's king, Philip II. The king had suffered a catastrophic and very embarrassing defeat at the hands of the English in 1588 with the Spanish Armada.

- The armada had had a disproportionate impact on the north of Ireland. In most parts of the country, the bedraggled Spanish sailors who actually made it to shore after braving the storms of the seas north of Scotland had simply been slaughtered. In Ulster, however, some 3,000 of them had been rescued and given shelter, and 500 of those made it over to Scotland. Anything involving a Spanish connection was going to set off loud alarm bells in the English administration.

The Rebellion

- The rebels had some early successes, but Hugh O'Neill was still on the fence, it seemed, trying hard to choose between his Irish compatriots and the English who had backed him against his O'Neill rivals. This is why the English could never entirely trust him.

- Hugh was in close touch with the Spanish court via one of Philip's agents. A government report on O'Neill summed up the English government's concern: "If [O'Neill's] purpose is to rebel it must proceed ... with a combination from Spain...his rebellion will be the more dangerous and cost the queen more crowns than any other that have foregone him since Her Majesty's reign."

- This prediction proved accurate in every respect. In the latter half of 1595, Hugh O'Neill quietly took over the reins of the conspiracy from Red Hugh O'Donnell, who had been the leader up until then. From this point on, O'Neill was in charge, though O'Donnell was his very close associate. O'Neill was a good commander. He was hampered in his campaigning by a lack of heavy artillery, but he countered this deficit by an effective use of guerilla tactics.

- The rebels wanted a type of autonomy for Ireland, but they accepted that Ireland would remain under the English crown. Religion also played a role, at least in the rhetoric of the rebels; they demanded that the church in Ireland be "wholly governed by the pope." That is, they effectively denied the royal supremacy. Under Elizabethan law, that was clearly treason.

- The result was the biggest, most unified rebellion in the 400 plus years of English rule in Ireland, and the campaigning took place over a far wider area of Ireland than ever before. Queen Elizabeth first sent Robert Devereux, earl of Essex, to crush the rebellion with 16,000 troops, but instead Devereux made a truce with O'Neill.

Mountjoy

- Elizabeth wasn't happy. Devereux was summoned home, where he started a rebellion himself as soon as he landed on English soil. He was caught and subsequently executed. Next, Elizabeth sent Charles Blount, also known as Lord Mountjoy, to attack O'Neill. Mountjoy wanted to isolate O'Neill in Ulster by building forts at key locations, hoping to starve O'Neill into submission.

Lord Mountjoy

- O'Neill knew that Mountjoy was going to be a lot tougher as an opponent than Essex had been, so he redoubled efforts that had been underway for some time to recruit help from Spain. In January of 1601, Philip III of Spain, who had succeeded his father three years earlier, promised to send 6,000 men to Ireland. But due to various setbacks, by the time the fleet landed on September 21 at Kinsale, just south and west of Cork City, there were fewer than 4,000 troops on board. When they landed, the local rebels had already been defeated. Given the lack of immediate local support, the Spanish commander, Don Juan del Águila, decided to hunker down inside Kinsale and wait for O'Neill to join him.

- Mountjoy moved in to besiege Kinsale, but O'Neill rushed south from Ulster to try to meet up with his Spanish allies. Mountjoy's army now had the rebels on one side and the Spanish garrison on the other. O'Neill attacked, but the maneuver he tried to pull off proved too confusing for his troops. It came down to a straight-out fight between the cavalry of both sides, and Mountjoy prevailed. The Spanish never came out of their fortress, and after negotiating for a week or so, they finally surrendered on January 2, 1602.

- The defeat at Kinsale was the beginning of the end. Hugh O'Neill's army made its way very laboriously back to Ulster, in terrible weather. O'Donnell went off to Spain to seek for more help, unsuccessfully. He died there, possibly of poison.

- Hugh O'Neill knew he was effectively beaten. He merely went underground as his supporters gradually trickled in to sue for pardon from the English, including Rory O'Donnell, the brother of his old compatriot. By the beginning of 1603, Elizabeth just wanted it all over, so she gave Mountjoy authorization to offer O'Neill life, liberty, and a pardon.

- In March of 1603, O'Neill agreed. He hung on for four more years, hoping that he would be able to reach an accommodation with the English regime, but in the end, it proved impossible. He and several companions went into exile in 1607.

More English Activities

- The ensuing so-called flight of the earls can be said with some oversimplification to represent the end of the old Irish order. After departing from Lough Swilly in the north of Ireland, the Irish lords traced a path through all the major Catholic countries of western Europe. They finally landed in Rome. The pope gave them pensions that were generous enough to allow them to live like gentlemen.

- O'Donnell died in July 1608 and was buried in the church of San Pietro di Montorio on the Janiculum Hill. O'Neill lived on, watched constantly by English agents. He never made it back to Ireland, and when he died in 1616, he was buried beside O'Donnell in Rome, where his grave can still be seen today.

- The English extended the policy of plantation to Ulster. The English government was determined to dilute the Irishness of this most rebellious province by importing settlers from England and the nearby Scottish Lowlands.

- The Scots of the Lowlands were very different from the Scots of the Highlands. The Lowlanders did not have linguistic or ethnic ties to Ireland. They were speakers of a dialect of English known as Scots, which descended from the language spoken in northern England in the Anglo-Saxon period. Many of them were ethnically the same as the English, though they had adopted a Scottish political identity.

- By this point, that Scottish political identity brought with it a fervent commitment to a very strong branch of reformed Protestantism, strongly Calvinist in outlook, that was based on the work of John Knox. They were utterly opposed to the Catholic faith. The Protestant, English-speaking Scots and Englishmen were not going to mix very well with the Catholic, Irish-speaking Irish. There were also some Scots settlers from the Gaelic-speaking western islands of Scotland, but the English government made sure that they were staunch Protestants.

Suggested Reading

Ellis, *Tudor Ireland*.

Ó Báoill, "Bardic Poetry."

Simms, *From Kings to Warlords*.

Spenser, *A View of the State of Ireland*.

Questions to Consider

1. What role did the clash of Irish and English cultures play in the Tudor conquest of Ireland?

2. How did native Irish lords attempt to navigate the two worlds they inhabited, Irish and English?

Lecture

21

(Re)Discovering the Celts

This lecture transitions from focusing on the Celts themselves to the ways in which Celtic heritage was rediscovered by scholars and reappropriated by people in the Celtic areas who believed that connecting with the Celtic past had meaning for them in the present. Modern notions of Celtic so-called nationalism all derive from this scholarly tradition that began in the 16th century. This lecture takes a look at such scholarship and at Celtic revivals in Scotland and Wales.

Scholarship

- As the English were finally conquering Ireland, scholars were uncovering the relationships between the Celtic languages, and several important translations of supposedly ancient Celtic texts took the European literary world by storm. The Celtic phenomenon thus became wildly popular among non-Celtic speakers only after any conceivable military threat from actual Celts had largely disappeared.

- The story of the intersection between scholarship and the Celts begins in the late 16th century with a Scottish scholar named George Buchanan. He was the first to discover the linguistic relationship among the Celtic languages and to popularize the notion of a so-called Celtic race.

- A native speaker of Scottish Gaelic, Buchanan was also a phenomenally talented linguist who wrote prolifically in both Latin and Scots, the form of English spoken in Scotland. Buchanan decided to investigate the origins of the Scots (and, by extension, the Irish) on his own terms.

- To do this, he invented a scholarly methodology, which was to investigate similarities in language, religion, and especially place names among several different peoples. He identified place names with common elements, such as the Lug- prefix that we see in places all over Europe; that prefix probably indicates a common cult of the god Lugh. This kind

George Buchanan

of evidence helped Buchanan piece together the theory that the Celtic speakers of the British Isles were related to the Celtic speakers of continental Europe.

- He didn't get everything right, but the biggest contribution Buchanan made was clearly to make a connection between Britain and the Continent and to say these were all Celts. This gave the Celtic speakers of Scotland a credibility that was rather important in an age when the Celtic languages were under assault. Suddenly, Buchanan's fellow Celts were related to the people who had almost successfully defied Julius Caesar.

Linguistic Progress

- Scholarly progress on Celtic linguistics took place in the Brythonic world with the work of a French scholar named Paul-Yves Pezron, who lived from 1639 to 1706. Pezron was a Cistercian monk from Brittany, so he was familiar with the Breton language.

- In 1703, he published a book entitled *Antiquité de la Nation et de la langue celtes autrement appelez Gaulois*, which was translated into English three years later as *The Antiquities of Nations; More Particularly of the Celtae or Gauls*. Pezron saw similarities between the Celtic languages and Greek and Latin.

- Pezron was reaching toward the methodology of comparative linguistics. He believed Breton was the last remnant of Gaulish, which he thought was derived from a language spoken at the time of the Tower of Babel. This was not exactly right, since Breton was actually the speech of the immigrants from Britain who had arrived in Brittany in the 5th century, but he was at least in the right ballpark. In fact, one of his most important contributions was to identify the connection between Breton and Welsh languages. From now on, the Welsh were seen to be Celts.

- When Pezron's work was translated into English, it was a Welshman who continued the progress: Edward Lhuyd, who lived from 1660 to 1709. Lhuyd compared vocabulary words from Welsh, Irish, Scottish Gaelic, Cornish, and Breton, and his great contribution was to bring all the Celtic languages together for the first time. He personally did not want to use the term *Celtic* for the languages of the British Isles and Ireland, but he did see the relationships between them, and he made a crucial discovery.

- Lhuyd was the first to recognize the sound changes between Welsh and Irish, that is the distinction between Q-Celtic and P-Celtic we discussed in an earlier lecture. Lhuyd also invented the terms *Goidelic* and *Brythonic* for the speakers of Q-Celtic and P-Celtic respectively, after characters in *The Book of Invasions*.

The Jacobites

- Scholarly work on the Celtic languages crossed over into popular culture in the 18th century in a huge way, partly driven by current events involving the Jacobites. The Jacobites were the fanatical, romantic faction that supported the exiled Stuart family, the descendants of James VII of Scotland and II of England, who had been driven from both the English and Scottish thrones in 1688 for being incompetent and gratuitously offensive to their subjects.

- A brief spoiler alert: the Jacobites ultimately lost, but between 1689 and 1745, there was a series of attempts, some of them more well developed than others, to restore the Stuarts to the British throne. The last attempt ended in April 1746 with the catastrophic defeat at the Battle of Culloden.

- The British government's reaction to the Jacobite uprising of 1745 had very important ramifications for the story of the Celts. The Battle of Culloden is often popularly believed to have been a clash between Highlanders on the Jacobite side and Lowlanders and Englishmen on the government side. This is emphatically not the case. There were speakers of Scottish Gaelic on both sides of the conflict.

- However, the British government associated all Highlanders with rebels, and they decided to carry out the kind of Anglicizing policy that had been pursued in Ireland at the time of the Tudor conquest there. They wanted to get the people to look and act more like Englishmen, or at least Lowland Scots.

- In 1746, the British passed the Dress Act of 1746, which banned the use of tartan, the distinctive multicolored checked cloth worn in the Highlands, except for Scottish regiments within the British army. By forbidding the wearing of tartan for civilians in 1746, the English were almost inevitably creating a mystique around tartan, and the odd effect seems to have been to expand the meaning of tartan from a marker of Highland or Gaelic identity to a marker of Scottish identity writ large.

A Literary Debate

- Tartan was not the only phenomenon that was controversial in the 18th century, as shown by one of the most famous literary debates of all time. It concerns a series of poems published beginning in 1760 by the Scottish poet James Macpherson, who claimed that they were translations from an ancient book written in Gaelic.

- The poems drew on tales familiar from Irish tradition, such as the stories from the Finn cycle about the great hero Finn MacCool and his son Ossian, who travels across the sea to the Otherworld with his fairy lover, only to return and discover that 300 years have passed in Ireland in what seemed to him the blink of an eye. Ossian is cast as the bardic narrator of the poems. They also include references to the Ulster cycle stories about the hero Cú Chulainn.

- The general public fell hard for Ossian. However, some members of the literary establishment began to raise questions right away. Irish people were angry that these texts were claimed for Scotland. But more seriously, doubts were raised about the authenticity of the poems: Where were the original texts on which these so-called translations were based? Macpherson never produced them.

- These days, the modern scholarly consensus is that Macpherson really did draw on original sources, but they were mostly oral. He gathered lots of ballads that contained traditional stories, many of which drew on traditions common to both Ireland and Scotland, and created an epic with many of his own touches.

Tartan Revival

- The Ossian craze helped to drive a renewed fascination with all things Scottish. In 1778, the Highland Society was founded in London so that expatriate Scots could get together and talk about Scottish culture.

- The profile of Scottish culture was raised even higher in 1782, when lobbying efforts by a Scottish nobleman led to the repeal of the Highland Dress Act. By that time, it was fairly clear that the Jacobites were no longer a threat.

- A fascinating twist occurred next. Before, tartan was a local marker; people wore the tartan of their locality. But after the 36-year hiatus in which local traditions were abrogated came a period of tartan revival and Highland chic; now, tartan was associated with particular clans. The Highland Society in 1815 mandated a tartan for each clan. Note that an organization in London was now presuming to tell Scottish clans what their proper tartans should be.

- Regardless, the tartan phenomenon thrived. A person who takes a huge amount of the credit is, ironically, a Lowland Scot who spoke no Gaelic: the famous Scottish poet and novelist Sir Walter Scott. In 1820, he founded the Celtic Society of Edinburgh, which put on a huge festival in 1822. Scots were urged to come "all plaided and plumed in their tartan array."

- Being a Lowlander, Scott's ancestors had surely never worn tartan. But somehow, the tartan had now become associated with Scottishness in general, as opposed to Highland Scottishness in particular. The tartan phenomenon got a huge boost when King George IV visited the festival in 1822 and appeared fully outfitted in royal Stuart tartan.

Wales

- At the same time that Scottish culture was tending in a decidedly Celtic direction, a Celtic revival was underway in Wales as well. It began in the mid-18th century with a renewed fascination with the druids. This had ironically been touched off first by an English vicar named William Stukeley, who first proposed the idea that the druids had worshiped in stone monuments like Stonehenge and Avebury (which we now know is not true).

- A much earlier German writer had already suggested that druids wore white robes (for which we have no evidence whatsoever), and the idea stuck. The druid craze spread to Wales, and the first druid society was founded on the Welsh island of Anglesey in 1772.

- At the same time as the druids were getting going again, there was a serious effort to revive the old traditions of the Welsh bards. Back in 1176, a powerful Welsh ruler called the Lord Rhys of Deheubarth had held a poetry competition at his court at Cardigan. Such an event was called an *eisteddfod*, which in Welsh means "session." These competitions continued during the Middle Ages, but they fell into abeyance in the 17th century. Then they were revived in 1789, when Thomas Jones created an event that was opened to the public for the first time.

- The most famous figure in the Welsh revival was Iolo Morganwg, who was interested in both poetry and druids. In 1792, Morganwg founded the Gorsedd Beirdd Ynys Prydain, an organization for the bards of the island of Britain, to put the revived eisteddfod on a sound footing.

- Morganwg was also an author. Note: Although Morganwg claimed to be publishing ancient Welsh texts, he clearly forged many of his manuscripts. Morganwg was very determined to prove continuity with the ancient druids and ancient bards, and in some cases, he went a bit too far. In 1789, he forged poems by the very famous 14th-century Welsh poet Dafydd ap Gwilym.

- However, the music and poetry on offer at the modern National Eisteddfod of Wales is not fake in the least. The Eisteddfod continues, and today it is considered one of the key cultural institutions of Wales.

Suggested Reading

Collis, *The Celts*, pp. 34–56.
Davies, *A History of Wales*, chapter 7.
Forsyth, *Bonnie Prince Charlie and the Jacobites*.
Macpherson, *Ossian's Fingal*.
Trevor-Roper, "The Invention of Tradition."
Wormald, *Scotland*, chapters 6–7.

Questions to Consider

1. How did the concept of the Celt develop during the early modern period?

2. How "authentic" are the "revived" Celtic traditions of Wales and Scotland?

Lecture
22

The Gaelic Revival in Ireland

The previous lecture discussed the Celtic revival movement in Wales and Scotland. In this lecture, we're going to continue to look at the Celtic revival, but this time, we'll be concentrating specifically on Ireland. In Ireland, the reappropriation of Celtic literature and art was more politically oriented than in Scotland and Wales. This identification with the Irish past manifested itself differently for different people. In order to understand the relationship between the Celtic revival and Irish politics, we need to catch up quickly on Irish political developments in the 19th century, and then we'll look at the four areas where Celtic revivalism was most important in Ireland: sports, language, art, and literature.

Political Background

- The 19th century in Ireland was dominated by a debate over the future of Ireland's relationship with Britain. In 1798, there was a major rebellion in Ireland led by a group called the United Irishmen, who were an explicitly nonsectarian, republican group. They wanted a democratic government for all of Ireland that was totally separate from Britain, but they really saw themselves as part of an international movement. They were very influenced by both the American Revolution and the French Revolution.

- The leader of the United Irishmen, a man called Theobald Wolfe Tone, was a Protestant lawyer from Dublin who had spent considerable time in Belfast. The nationalism of the United Irishmen was supposed to transcend religion and certainly to transcend ethnicity.

- The British government saw the rebellion of 1798 as a very serious threat to national security because it led to French troops landing on Irish soil, and even though these troops were very quickly defeated, the British wanted to be sure that such an invasion never happened again.

- Until this time, the Irish had had their own parliament, but in 1800, the Act of Union did away with the Irish Parliament and brought Ireland under the direct rule of the British Parliament in London. This was supposed to help with security, and the British government also promised that an all-British governing body would be in a better position to guarantee the rights of Catholics in Ireland than the local Protestant landlords in Ireland. At the time, many Catholics in Ireland, including the Catholic bishops, backed the union.

- Fairly quickly after the passage of the Act of Union, it became clear that the new constitutional arrangement was more beneficial for some groups in Ireland than others. The more heavily industrialized northeast of the country, which had been settled extensively by Protestant Scots and Englishmen in the 17th century, did very well.

- The rest of the country, which was more heavily Catholic, failed to see the economic gains they had expected. Disenchantment with the union only increased due to the catastrophic effects of the Great Famine of the 1840s, when the potato crop failed repeatedly, leading to widespread death from starvation and disease and massive emigration.

- Throughout the 19th century, then, there was a lively debate over the best way for Ireland to express its relationship with Britain. There were three main strands of opinion. The first was unionism—that is—the belief that the Act of Union was a good thing. Most unionists were Protestants who identified strongly with Britain.

- There were also two strands of nationalist opinion. The less radical one was constitutional nationalism. The constitutional nationalists wanted to see Ireland recover at least some of the political autonomy it had had before the Act of Union while remaining connected to Britain in some way. There were prominent constitutional nationalists from both the Protestant and Catholic communities.

- In fact, the two most famous Irish politicians of the 19th century came from opposite sides of the religious divide. The Catholic Daniel O'Connell, who died in 1847, led a successful effort to repeal the law that barred Catholics from serving in political office. He failed in his campaign to get the Act of Union repealed and restore the Irish Parliament. I'll say more about O'Connell's relationship to the Irish language and Irish history a bit later on.

- The Protestant Charles Stewart Parnell was an ardent Irish patriot who built on O'Connell's work by working toward the slightly less ambitious goal of achieving home rule for Ireland. Parnell came very close to achieving this goal, but he was brought down in 1890 by his adulterous relationship with a woman named Kitty O'Shea; many public figures condemned Parnell, including the Catholic bishops of Ireland. The Parnell scandal split the constitutional nationalist community, and it was another two decades before home rule came to the top of the political agenda again.

Daniel O'Connell

- A far smaller and more radical fringe of the nationalist movement wanted an absolute rupture of any ties to Great Britain achieved by means of an armed struggle. They became known as the Fenians, and this was a direct reference to the ancient Irish Fianna, the warrior band of Finn MacCool.

- Within the nationalist community, there were several main areas of emphasis. Some worked most intensively on political change, while others concentrated on trying to improve the economic situation for Irish farmers. Still others devoted their energies into a movement to shore up the Irishness of Ireland by preserving and reviving its distinctive cultural heritage. This effort proceeded on several fronts, from athletics to language, literature, and art; many people were involved in more than one of these areas.

Sports

- The first of these organized movements was devoted to the revival of ancient Irish sports. The ancient Irish sport that we have the most evidence for is hurling. In the Irish epic *Táin*, there are references to the hero Cú Chulainn playing a game with the boy troop at the royal court of Ulster that involved striking a ball with a stick. We also know that it was played in the Middle Ages, because it was one of the Irish games that the English settlers were banned from playing under the Statutes of Kilkenny in 1366.

- We know less about the other main Irish sport that was revived in the 19th century, namely, Gaelic football. Both hurling and football, though, were in decline by the middle of the 19th century due to competition from sports brought in from England, especially soccer and cricket.

- In response, the Gaelic Athletic Association, or GAA, was founded on November 1, 1884, by a teacher from County Clare named Michael Cusack in the billiard room at Hayes Hotel in Thurles. One of the other key sponsors of the new organization was Thomas William Croke, archbishop of Cashel.

- Archbishop Croke was one of the casualties of the Parnell divorce scandal. After the scandal broke, he became disillusioned and withdrew from active politics, but he left a lasting legacy in the GAA. The GAA stadium in Dublin, Croke Park, is named after him.

- Croke Park was the site of one of the most notorious episodes of the Irish War of Independence in 1920, when members of the British special troops known as the Black and Tans fired on the spectators at a Gaelic football match. The attack was launched in retaliation for a series of assassinations of British security officers that had taken place that morning under the orders of the director of intelligence for the Irish Republican Army, Michael Collins.

- The attack killed 14 civilians. There was clear symbolism in attacking a GAA match, because by this period, the GAA had become clearly identified with radical Irish republicanism. By the early 1900s, the Irish Republican Brotherhood, the radical group associated with the Fenian legacy, had heavily infiltrated the GAA. This is not to say that all GAA members were republicans, but many were.

Language

- Ironically, there was an upsurge of interest in the Irish language in the late 19th century just as it was largely dying out as a spoken language among the people of Ireland. The factors leading to its decline included the deadly potato famine of the 1840s and the repeal of the Penal Laws. From the 17th century onward, legislation known as the Penal Laws had restricted economic and political opportunities for Catholics in both Britain and Ireland, but once it was legal for Catholics in Ireland to join the professions, there was a much greater incentive for them to learn English.

- In the immediate aftermath of the famine, Ireland was preoccupied with survival and recovery. It took another generation before a movement arose that would try to undo the linguistic damage caused by famine, emigration, and assimilation. The organization that took on that challenge was the Gaelic League, or *Conradh na Gaeilge* in Irish, which was founded in 1893 by three men: Eugene O'Growney, Eoin MacNeill, and Douglas Hyde.

- The aim of the league was primarily to revive the Irish language at all levels and to introduce it into the national curriculum. The league also campaigned (often successfully) for bilingual street signs and signposts.

All over Ireland, there were people gathering together in local branches, learning Irish.

- The Gaelic League created an ideal of an Irish Ireland that was going to influence future nationalists very strongly. The league gained many more members after 1899 due to the outbreak of the Boer War between Britain and the Boer rebels in South Africa; many Irishmen sided with the Boers, and they joined the league as an expression of anti-British partisanship. Still, the league was officially non-political for quite some time.

- This officially non-political stance was maintained until 1915, when the Gaelic League finally committed itself to independence, at which point Douglas Hyde resigned. Many of the participants in the Easter Rising rebellion of 1916 were members of the Gaelic League. There was some tension among the rebels between those who were competent in spoken Irish and those who weren't. By that point, the ability to speak Irish had become a marker of Irish nationalist credibility.

Literature

- A broader approach to Gaelic revival focused on the actual literary heritage of Ireland, regardless of the language through which one might choose to encounter it. Most of the practitioners of this form of literary revival were members of the largely Protestant Anglo-Irish community. They sought their inspiration in old Irish mythology and folklore.

- The Anglo-Irish literary figure Augusta, Lady Gregory, for example, learned Old Irish. In 1902, she published *Cuchulain of Muirthemne*, a well-received translation of the *Táin*. She preserved most of the plot, but took out some of the stranger aspects of the original story.

- The most famous name associated with the Gaelic literary revival is that of William Butler Yeats. Yeats used many Irish settings for his poem, and he often drew on specific Irish myths and tales. Just as Macpherson was inspired by the stories of Ossian in the 18th century, Yeats wrote a poem about Ossian, except he didn't claim that he had found it in an ancient manuscript.

- Probably the most important works that the Gaelic revival produced were plays. Lady Gregory and Yeats cofounded the Irish Literary Theatre in 1899, later known as the Abbey Theatre, with the aim of producing Irish-themed plays.

Celtic Art

Lady Gregory

- The fascination with Celtic art has somewhat different origins from the movements in sports, language, and literature, but they became intertwined. The Celtic art movement was largely inspired by the advances in literary scholarship and archaeology in the 19th century. Antiquarian scholars were translating ancient Irish manuscripts into English, in some cases for the first time. The *Book of Kells* became a symbol of Irish cultural preeminence; in 1849, when Queen Victoria and Prince Albert visited Ireland, they were asked to sign the *Book of Kells*.

- There were the spectacular discoveries of the Tara Brooch in 1850 and the Ardagh Chalice in 1868, among others. They inspired contemporary jewelry and metalwork. Queen Victoria loved the Tara Brooch so much that she had it copied to be given as gifts. At the same time, archaeologists were working out their theory of the origins of the Celts at Hallstatt and La Tène, so all of this art was seen as connecting Ireland to a great continental tradition.

- The greatest impact of the revival in Celtic art was in applied arts, such as book illustration and home furnishings, where we see a huge flowering of traditional Celtic motifs such as geometric designs, knotwork, and interlaced animals. These Celtic motifs were used prolifically in the printed materials put out by the Gaelic League and the GAA, as well as in the programs and posters of the Abbey Theatre. Irish cultural nationalism had a distinctively Celtic look.

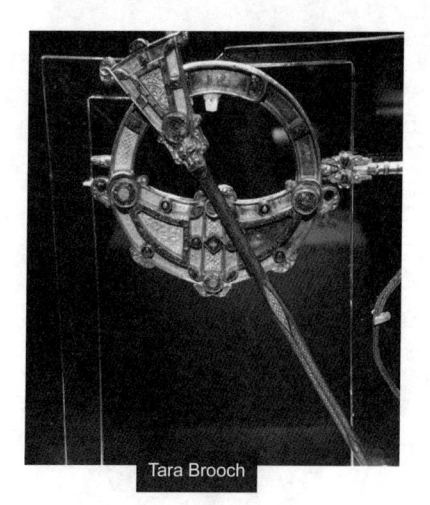

Tara Brooch

Suggested Reading

Augusta, *Cuchulain of Muirthemne*.
Collis, *The Celts*, chapter 5.
Conradh na Gaeilge (Gaelic League), https://www.cnag.ie/en/.
Gaelic Athletic Association, http://www.gaa.ie/.
MacManus, *The Story of the Irish Race*.
O'Connor, *All the Olympians*.
Synge, *The Complete Plays*.
Yeats, *Eleven Plays of William Butler Yeats*.

Questions to Consider

1. How did the Gaelic revival make use of ancient Irish traditions to create a modern Celtic identity?

2. In what senses did the movement to revive the Irish language both succeed and fail?

Lecture 23

Celtic Music and Dance

This lecture looks in detail at arguably the most influential living Celtic tradition today, namely, Celtic music and Celtic dance. Celtic music bridges the linguistic divide between Celtic peoples and substitutes, in some cases, for languages that have gone out of use, as in Galicia and other parts of northwest Spain. It is enormously popular around the world.

Early Music

- The earliest musical instrument that we know of that is associated with the peoples of Central Europe is the great Iron Age war trumpet known as the carnyx. We don't have physical remains of musical instruments from the Celtic regions for the early Middle Ages, but we do at least have some artistic representations. The Gauls put pictures of the U-shaped stringed instrument called the *lyre* on their coins.

- We also know something about the status of musicians in early Ireland, thanks to the Irish obsession with defining social status in a hierarchical manner. Musicians had a relatively high rank, and among musicians, harpers ranked the highest.

- English invaders of both Ireland and Wales very much distrusted native musicians. The English feared that bards would pass along a lot of seditious songs and also corrupt English settlers into assimilating into native culture. In Ireland, the famous Statutes of Kilkenny in 1366 specifically barred the English settlers from employing Irish musicians. Such was the attraction of Irish music, however, that the English settlers carried on employing Irish minstrels throughout the Middle Ages.

- Minstrels were also seen as a potentially disruptive element in Wales. In 1401, in the context of the great revolt of Owen Glendower, the English government of King Henry IV clamped down on all assemblies of Welshmen and specifically ordered that "wandering Welsh minstrels, bards, rhymers and wasters and 'other vagabonds' should be imprisoned."

- The earliest written description of Celtic music comes from one of the most anti-Celtic, or at least anti-Irish, works in history, namely, the *History and Topography of Ireland* by Gerald of Wales. Gerald had almost nothing good to say about the Irish, but he did appreciate their art, and he especially liked their music, which he described as "quick and lively."

- Gerald's praise of Irish music comes with a sting. He will allow that the Irish invented this music, but he claims that the Scots and the Welsh have now outstripped the Irish in this regard. This reveals something about Gerald's perceptions of how the Irish are related to the other peoples of the Celtic Fringe.

- Gerald looks down on the Irish for using only two instruments where the Scots and the Welsh use three. The Irish use the harp and the tympanum, or hand drum, he says. The Scots use three instruments: the harp, the tympanum, and the crowd, which is a kind of lyre played with a bow. The Welsh, he says, play the harp, the pipes, and the crowd. This seems a bit odd since today the Scots are more associated with the pipes than the Welsh are, and the crowd is now seen as a Welsh instrument, but Gerald is not to be trusted in every detail.

Characteristics of Celtic Music

- Throughout the Celtic-speaking regions, there is a strong emphasis on the ornamentation of the melody. This is what we might think of in classical music terms as the theme and variations.

- If the character of this music has some elements that have remained constant, the instruments used to play it have changed substantially over time. As Gerald noted, the quintessential early instrument in all the Celtic musical traditions that we know of was the harp.

- The tradition of the harpists was dealt a serious blow by the decline of the Irish aristocracy in the 17th century. No longer could a single noble family maintain its own retinue of poets and musicians. A few harpers hung on as itinerant musicians. This last gasp of the old tradition is best exemplified by the blind harpist Turliugh O'Carolan, who lived in the late 17th and early 18th centuries, and whose music is still played regularly today on a variety of instruments.

- Along with the previously mentioned tympanum and crowd, Gerard also describes the pipes, which are yet another example of something that came to the Celtic world from elsewhere and then developed into something distinctive. There are many different kinds of pipes, but most of them have several things in common.

- The first is the fact that they use enclosed reeds that are fed from a reservoir of air in a bag. The air can be provided by blowing through a blowpipe or by squeezing the bag with a bellows tucked under the upper arm. Most pipes also have a drone, which is a pipe that produces a single constant note that underlies the melody, which is itself played on the chanter. The drone gives the bagpipes a very distinctive sound.

- The bagpipes really took off in Scotland during the 16th century, when the large pipes that we know of today as the Highland bagpipes were used as a battlefield instrument. The Scottish scholar George Buchanan noted that bagpipes had replaced the trumpet on the battlefield.

- By the 16th century, the bagpipes had spread to Ireland, and there is even a contemporary illustration of the bagpipes used in a military context in Ireland dating to 1581. This cross-fertilization between Ireland and Scotland continued. Today, the bagpipes play an integral part in the traditions of American fire departments and police departments, many of which were dominated in the 19th and 20th centuries by Irish immigrants and their descendants.

- Aside from the characteristically Celtic instruments mentioned by Gerald of Wales, some kind of violin-like instrument was played in Ireland since at least the 8th century. The earliest surviving example dates to the 11th century. However, this medieval Irish fiddle died out. The European violin replaced it in the 18th century, and both Irish and Scottish music would now be hard to imagine without the fiddle.

- It would be equally hard to imagine Celtic music without the distinctive sound of the flute, tin whistle, or penny whistle. But whistles are an even more recent arrival on the Celtic music scene. They did not really start being played in Ireland until the 19th century, when they began to be mass-produced very cheaply in Manchester, England.

- Similarly, the accordion and concertina are also late-19th-century imports into this musical tradition. Today, we can add the banjo, bouzouki, mandolin, and guitar, among other instruments. The sound of Celtic music is always evolving.

Voice

- The human voice is one of the most important instruments used in Celtic music. There are several very distinctive singing styles that are vital to this tradition. A prominent one is an a cappella Irish style known as *sean nós*, which uses the Irish language.

- A very different vocal style is called lilting, which can be found in both Ireland and Scotland. Lilting is a bit like the Gaelic equivalent of scat, in which nonsense syllables are sung to a melody. Lilting could be used to accompany dancers as a substitute for a musical instrument if none were at hand.

- Another important Irish singing tradition is the ballad. These story songs grew out of the bardic tradition in Irish, but in the 19th century, songs began to be composed widely in English. Many were love songs, such as the beautiful "Star of the County Down."

- There is also a rich tradition of explicitly political songs in Ireland, on both the nationalist and the unionist sides. From the middle of the 20th century on, singing groups such as the Clancy Brothers, Tommy Makem, and the Dubliners made these songs popular around the world.

- While singing in the Gaelic world has emphasized solo performers until quite recently, the most famous form of singing from Wales is definitely choral singing. Notations of Welsh choral music appeared in the 18th century, which coincided with the Methodist revival movement. The Methodists privileged hymn singing over instrumental music because they regarded it as less decadent, and out of this tradition grew the very strong emphasis on the male voice choir.

Dancing

- One of the other musical impacts of the Methodist revival in Wales was a decline in traditional Welsh dancing, about which we know much less than we would like. It is far more to Ireland and Scotland that we need to look for the origins of the dance traditions that have proved so influential around the world.

- Unfortunately, we know even less about the origins of dancing in Ireland and Scotland than we do about music. There is less visual evidence that survives. The earliest mention of dancing in Ireland is actually from a famous 14th-century Middle English poem that calls on the listener to "come aunt daunce wyt me in Irlaunde."

- In the 16th century, when all kinds of written sources increase tremendously, we suddenly have lots of references to dancing. Various kinds of dances are mentioned, including the "hay," the "fading," and the "trenchmore," though we have no idea what these dances looked like. Dancing was reportedly very popular among the poorer classes, especially at agricultural festivals.

- Irish and Scottish dance came into focus in the 18th century, at the same time as the violin was introduced. The most important dance meters were the jig and the reel. The jig is in a triple meter, with either two or three groups of three notes. A jig with three groups of three notes is called a slip jig. The reel is in double or quadruple meter, and it's usually a rapid melody with an emphasis on eighth notes. There are usually two related melodic parts that are repeated in various patterns.

- One specifically Scottish dance is the strathspey. In contrast to the reel, it is slow and stately, characterized by a very distinctive rhythm called the Scotch snap, which is a short note before a longer note.

- Today, Irish dancing in particular has become a worldwide phenomenon thanks to the success of the show *Riverdance* and its spinoff, Michael Flatley's *Lord of the Dance*. These dance extravaganzas draw on the tradition of Irish dance, but it's important to note that Irish dance as we know it today is a relatively recent phenomenon.

To the Present

- The traditions discussed in this lecture went into decline even in Ireland in the 19th century, particularly under the withering criticism of the Catholic Church. The decline lasted until late in the century, when the Gaelic League decided to help revive Irish music and dance just as it was attempting to revive the Irish language. The late 19th century also saw the beginning of the tradition of decorating dancers' costumes with explicitly Celtic motifs, to the point that many Irish dancers' dresses today look almost exactly like carpet pages from the *Book of Kells*.

- However, just as the learned revival of the language attempted to introduce some standardization amidst linguistic diversity, the revival of dance led to a rather rigid codification of norms. Irish step dancing is characterized by the very distinctive emphasis on the rigid posture of the upper body so that all of the focus is placed on the movement of the feet. This is not a feature of Scottish dance, which is otherwise somewhat similar to Irish dance, so presumably, at one point the two forms were more similar.

- There are traditionalists and avant-gardists in any art form, and Celtic music and dance are no exception. Many groups today fuse traditional Celtic musical forms with new instrumentation.

Relations

- The musical traditions of Ireland, Scotland, and Wales influenced each other. There is not as close a relationship between these regions and Brittany and Galicia, but if anything, the Celtic music scene in the Celtic regions of France and Spain is more explicitly pan-Celtic. For example, take the Interceltic Festival at Lorient in Brittany and the Interceltic Festival of Avilés in the Spanish autonomous region of Asturias, an aspirational Celtic community that is trying to get accepted into the club.

- The idea of being part of a wider musical community that represents an ancient kinship is a very powerful one. It is nicely encapsulated in a piece by the Irish composer Shaun Davey called "The Pilgrim." The piece was commissioned in 1983 for the Glasgow Royal Concert Hall to mark the transfer of the title of European Culture City from Glasgow to Dublin. The conceit is that St. Columba goes on a voyage from Ireland through all the other Celtic countries, including Galicia. It uses musicians from all the Celtic countries, so the audience actually hears the kinship between the Celtic regions.

- Music from Scotland and Ireland has also had an impact on music in the United States, where immigrants from Scotland and Ulster settled in the Appalachian Mountains and strongly influenced bluegrass and country music. Additionally, in the Canadian Maritimes, the Scots put down roots on Cape Breton Island. Irish immigrants mingled with the French settlers in Quebec to create a distinctive musical fusion that is uniquely Québécois.

Suggested Reading

Gerald of Wales, *The History and Topography of Ireland*, pp. 103–104.
Ó hAllmhuráin, *A Short History of Irish Traditional Music*.
Ritchie and Orr, *Wayfaring Strangers*.

Questions to Consider

1. In what ways has modern Celtic music preserved ancient traditions, and in what ways has it been transformed?

2. What explains the appeal of Celtic music and dance?

Lecture

24

The Celts Today

It is not a simple matter to draw a direct line between the ancient Celts and the Celts of today. However, modern inhabitants of the Celtic regions have made a conscious effort to connect with their ancestors. The Celts of the past and modern Celts do have certain things in common, especially practices that have made Celtic culture so popular around the world, such as a pronounced love for literature and music, art, and even sports. This final lecture presents an overview of the Celtic world today. First, the lecture looks at the Celtic phenomenon as a whole by tracing the history of the so-called pan-Celtic movement over the past century or so. Then, the lecture discusses the individual Celtic regions comparatively and considers two related topics: politics and language.

Questions of Celtic identity are still salient in political debates today, including the movements for regional autonomy in Brittany and Galicia, the ongoing political struggle in Northern Ireland, and the debate over Scottish independence. There is no single response to these questions.

The Pan-Celtic Movement

- The origins of the pan-Celtic movement date to the late 19th century, at the same time as the Gaelic revival in Ireland. Like the Gaelic revival, pan-Celticism was part of the wider European romantic nationalist current that included movements such as pan-Slavism.

- In 1900, the Celtic Association was formed to promote Celtic culture, and it began holding frequent pan-Celtic congresses. These meetings included some of the trappings of Celtic revivalism looked at in an earlier lecture. For example, congresses would open with neo-druidic ceremonies.

- Some of the more radical proponents of pan-Celticism, such as the Celtic League, founded in 1961, actually want to unite the Celtic realms under a single, Celtic political authority. This would mean that all of the Celtic realms except the Republic of Ireland would need to secede from the nation states of which they are currently a part. There is no realistic chance of any such unified Celtic state ever materializing. Nevertheless, the Celtic League is a United Nations–accredited non-governmental organization.

- One of the political undercurrents of pan-Celticism is resistance to an imperial authority, whether it be in London, Paris, or Madrid. Modern pan-Celticists thus draw an analogy between the resistance to Rome by the ancient Celts and their own resistance to centralizing authority today. Such an analogy is full of problems, but this is a clear case where pan-Celticists have found a usable past.

- Over the past century or so, the pan-Celtic movement has faced a serious issue: defining what Celtic means. The number of areas that claim Celtic associations is constantly expanding. The first pan-Celtic congress included just five Celtic realms: Ireland, Brittany, Wales, Scotland, and the Isle of Man. Not until 1904 did Cornwall manage to claw its way into the linguistically minded congress; it faced opposition at first because of the moribund status of the Cornish language. Galicia has never made it into the association because there really is no viable Galician Celtic language.

- There is even a small movement to recognize Switzerland as a Celtic nation, since Celtic speakers once inhabited it. One manifestation of this movement is the Swiss folk metal band Eluveitie, whose songs frequently deal with Celtic mythology; the lyrics are often in a reconstructed form of ancient Gaulish.

Language

- It's fair to say that the issues of who is in and who is out of the Celtic club do not preoccupy the vast majority of people in the Celtic regions.

Instead, the Celtic question comes up most frequently regarding debates over political autonomy and language policy.

- For example, take the Isle of Man. It has been a cultural melting pot through the centuries and has changed hands numerous times, but since the 14th century, it has been ruled by England, though its status is a bit peculiar. The Isle of Man is not governed directly by the United Kingdom's Parliament. Instead, it has considerable autonomy for internal affairs, while the British government handles defense and external matters.

- Since 1985, Manx has been one of the two official languages of the Isle of Man, even though in the 2011 census, only about two percent of the Manx population of 85,000 claimed to be able to speak the Manx language. Road signs are bilingual throughout the island, and some broadcasting is available in Manx.

- The next largest of the Celtic regions is Cornwall. Cornwall participated in the 19th-century Celtic revival, but by that point, the Cornish language had largely died out. The marginal status of Cornwall and Cornish made it hard for the Cornish revival movement to get taken seriously by the larger Celtic powers.

- However, starting in the 1990s, affairs moved forward. There are now bilingual street signs in Cornwall, just as there are on the Isle of Man. There is a bilingual Cornish-English daycare center where parents also take special classes in Cornish so that they can reinforce the Cornish that their kids are learning. BBC Cornwall broadcasts a certain amount of Cornish, and books are increasingly available in Cornish. In 2011, the British census recorded 557 people who claimed Cornish as their main language, and 3,000 people claimed to be fluent.

- With regard to politics, there is a small movement that favors autonomy for Cornwall, largely on the basis of the Celtic heritage of the Cornish people, but it does not enjoy widespread support. Efforts to create a devolved legislative assembly for Cornwall on a par with the parliaments in Wales and Scotland have gained little traction.

Celtic Resonance in France

- The resonance of the Celts in France cuts in two directions. On the one hand, there is the legacy of the Gauls. This legacy has looked different at different points in French history.

- In the 19th century, the French were fascinated with all things Celtic. But the Celts had a quite different resonance in the mid-20th century. During the Vichy period, some people saw the defeat of the Gauls as a prudent and beneficial concession to the march of progress; thus, they argued the French should surrender to the Germans and join in a new and better Europe.

- Of course, not everyone agreed, and in the postwar years, a quite different picture of the relationship between Rome and the Gauls emerged. In 1959, *Asterix the Gaul*, written by René Goscinny and illustrated by Albert Uderzo, told the story of a Gaulish warrior who lives in the last village to hold out against Julius Caesar and the Romans, who are treated as buffoons. Asterix symbolizes resistance to outside forces; the Romans clearly stand in for the Nazis. The series now numbers more than 30 books.

- In these instances, the Gauls are used to help French people think about the relationship between France as a whole and its neighbors in the rest of Europe. But the Brittany question is quite different, because here the unity of France is at stake.

- The ambivalence of the relationship between Brittany and the rest of France can be seen in a very famous French family, the de Gaulles. Charles de Gaulle the elder, the uncle of the more famous French statesman, was a 19th-century writer who became fascinated by the pan-Celtic movement, learned Breton, and wrote Breton-language poetry.

- Fast forwarding to the 1960s, President Charles de Gaulle enacted a number of measures to crack down on Breton separatism. In 1968, while on a visit to Brittany to try to smooth things over, he tried to trade on his uncle's literary reputation by declaiming one of his Breton poems. Given that de Gaulle had recently agitated for independence for Quebec on the grounds of linguistic tradition, de Gaulle's use of the Breton poem struck the hostile crowd as hypocritical, and they drowned out the rest of the speech.

Charles de Gaulle

- These days, Breton separatism is not very strong. Fewer than 20 percent of those polled in 2013 want Brittany to be independent, though many more than that would probably support greater autonomy from the central government. The Breton language, unfortunately, has undergone a steep decline in recent years. In the early 20th century, there were about 2 million Breton speakers, but as of 2007, the number had shrunk to about 200,000.

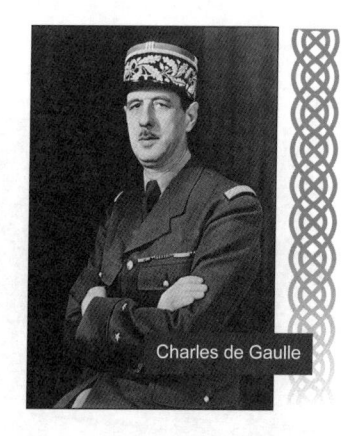

Wales and Scotland

- There is no particular correlation between the level of survival of the Celtic languages and the level of separatist sentiment. Wales has by far the highest proportion of Celtic-language speakers of any of the Celtic realms. The 2011 census showed 562,000 Welsh-speakers, making up about 19 percent of the population. This is by far the largest number of speakers of any Celtic language anywhere.

- This is partly due to the strong support for Welsh in the schools. All Welsh students take Welsh in school until at least age 14. Bilingual street signs in Welsh and English have been standard throughout Wales since the 1970s. Nevertheless, the Welsh are markedly less separatist than the Irish or the Scots. The Welsh nationalist party has never managed to seize control of Welsh local politics the way the Scottish National Party has in Scotland.

- The Welsh were granted their own legislative assembly in 1998 (since upgraded to a parliament) on a much narrower referendum vote than the Scots. Wales voted 50.3 percent in favor of devolution versus 49.7 percent against, in contrast to the Scots, who voted 74 percent to 26 percent in favor. In September 2014, Scotland held a second referendum, this time on independence, which ended in a convincing victory for the no vote.

The Irish Language

- The Irish language played a very large part in the rise of Irish nationalism. Many nationalists who never attained much fluency in Irish nevertheless paid lip service at the very least to the desirability of reviving Irish, and in the early years of the Irish Free State in the 1920s, a serious effort was made to make Irish the everyday language of the people. The use of Irish as a mark of identity is controversial to this day.

- Today, enormous resources are poured into supporting the Irish language. Nevertheless, the number of active users of Irish stubbornly refuses to climb, despite the fact that the Irish language is compulsory for all Irish schoolchildren and a mandatory subject in the Leaving Certificate exam. The major political parties in Ireland have periodically gotten into hot water if they seemed to waver at all in their support for the Irish language, which is often seen as a measure of patriotism.

- Irish-language policy can be controversial in the Republic of Ireland, but it is even more politically sensitive in Northern Ireland. In the republic, there is at least broad consensus that there is a connection between the Irish language and Irish identity; even people who really resent having to learn Irish might feel a bit guilty about doing so.

- However, in Northern Ireland, where the population is divided between people who identify themselves primarily as Irish and people who identify themselves primarily as British, there is a long history of Irish being used as a marker of radical nationalism. For example, during the Troubles of the 1960s through the 1980s, some of the most popular classes available to nationalist prisoners were Irish-language courses. Happily, Northern Ireland is now at peace, though many issues remain to be solved, including issues of identity that are partially expressed by means of language.

Sports in Ireland

- Language is not the only cultural issue that divides north and south in Ireland. Another very salient issue is sports. The Gaelic Athletic Association (GAA) is central to the national identity of the Republic of

Ireland, and it's woven into the political fabric of the nation. For male Irish politicians in particular, it can be a huge asset to have played GAA sports for their county.

- The reason the GAA is controversial politically is that GAA games are played as county-versus-county competitions in all 32 counties of the island of Ireland. In certain strongly nationalist neighborhoods of Belfast, such as the Ardoyne, highly sectarian murals celebrate the nationalist credentials of the GAA. The GAA is so nationalist that until quite recently, members of the GAA were forbidden to play so-called foreign games, which really meant sports that had been introduced into Ireland from England. That included soccer, rugby, and cricket.

Summing Up

- Summing up over 2,000 years of the Celtic phenomenon is a tall order, but it's useful to give it a try. A specific question can help: Who are the Celts, and what can modern DNA analysis tell us about their origins?

- Recent work has shown that the residents of the so-called Celtic Fringe had probably been living in these areas for thousands of years before the people known to the classical authors as the Celts were active on the continent. DNA can fairly conclusively refute the old Celtic hypothesis about a Celtic invasion of Britain and Ireland.

- Some scholars have suggested that since the people the Romans and the Greeks knew as the Celts are clearly not the same people as the residents of Ireland and Britain, it is now time to get rid of the word *Celtic* altogether. This course's view is that this is the right approach.

- The word *Celtic* has many meanings. Even if there were no particular genetic connections between the Celts of the continent and the British Isles and Ireland, there were clearly many connections in art, language, and culture. People can share a culture and even a language without sharing DNA.

- The same cultural fluidity that operated in the ancient world is even more prevalent today. Celtic culture is not the province of any one ethnic group; it is there to be embraced by anyone who is inspired by great art, literature, and music, and by the fascinating story of the relationship between peoples who were marginalized politically but nevertheless had a disproportionate impact on world culture.

- Today, there are St. Patrick's Day parades not just in almost every state in the United States and every country in Europe, but in China, Japan, and Singapore as well. The World Pipe Band Championships held in Glasgow attract bagpipers from around the world. Whiskey, or *uisce beatha* (the "water of life"), has never been more popular, in both its Irish version (spelled with an e) and its Scottish version (spelled without).

- But the Celts are about more than parades and bagpipes and whiskey. The Celtic story is also about the persistence of art and creativity in the face of adversity, and as such, this course's view is that it belongs to people of all backgrounds. The Celtic world is for everyone.

Suggested Reading

Celtic Congress, http://www.celtic-congress.org/.

Celtic League, https://www.celticleague.net/.

Collis, *The Celts*, chapters 9–11.

Galliou and Jones, *The Bretons*, chapter 14.

Ghosh, "DNA Study Shows Celts Are Not a Unique Genetic Group."

Goscinny and Uderzo, *Asterix the Gaul*.

Ryan, "Taoiseach Defends Appointment of Minister without Fluent Irish."

The Secret of Kells (film).

Whoriskey, "A Man's Discovery of Bones under His Pub Could Forever Change What We Know about the Irish."

Questions to Consider

1. How should we assess the strength and authenticity of Celtic traditions in the modern world?

2. How, if at all, should modern scholarly controversies about the Celts affect participation in activities that are considered to be Celtic?

Bibliography

Adomnan of Iona. *Life of St. Columba*. Translated by Richard Sharpe. London: Penguin Books, 1995. Biography of one of the most important early Irish missionary saints.

Aldhouse-Green, Miranda. *Boudica Britannia: Rebel, War-Leader, and Queen*. Harlow: Pearson Education, 2006. A study of the archetypal Celtic woman warrior.

Augusta, Lady Gregory. *Cuchulain of Muirthemne*. Fifth edition. Gerrards Cross: Smythe, 1973. A translation of *The Táin* that greatly influenced the Gaelic revival in Ireland.

Ball, Martin J., and Nicole Müller. *The Celtic Languages*. London: Routledge, 1993. A thorough study of the Celtic family of languages, including its origins, by a series of experts.

Barrow, G. W. S. *Kingship and Unity: Scotland 1000–1306*. Toronto: University of Toronto Press, 1981. An elegant, concise study of the formation of the Scottish kingdom.

Bede. *Ecclesiastical History of the English People*. Translated by Leo Shirley-Price. Revised edition. London: Penguin Books, 1991. Includes the famous, if disputed, account of the Synod of Whitby in 664.

Binchy, Daniel. "Secular Institutions." In *Early Irish Society*, edited by Myles Dillon, pp. 52–64. Dublin: Cultural Relations Committee of Ireland, 1954. The source of Binchy's classic formulation that Ireland is "tribal, rural, hierarchical, and familiar."

Bitel, Lisa M. *Isle of the Saints: Monastic Settlement and Christian Community in Early Ireland.* Ithaca: Cornell University Press, 1994. A brilliant study of the role of monasteries in early Irish society.

———. *Land of Women: Tales of Sex and Gender from Early Ireland.* Ithaca: Cornell University Press, 1995. A provocative and innovative examination of the place of women in early Irish society.

———. "St. Brigid of Ireland: From Virgin Saint to Fertility Goddess." Monastic Matrix. http://monasticmatrix.osu.edu/commentaria/st-brigit-ireland. A persuasive argument in favor of the view that St. Brigid was a real person whose biographers increasingly portrayed as a Celtic goddess.

Caesar, Julius. *The Conquest of Gaul.* Translated by S. A. Handford. London: Penguin Books, 1983. Caesar's memoirs of his campaigns in Gaul, written in the third person.

Cahill, Thomas. *How the Irish Saved Civilization: The Untold Story of Ireland's Heroic Role from the Fall of Rome to the Rise of Medieval Europe.* New York: Anchor Books, 1995. A bestselling study of the Irish role in early medieval scholarship that engages in some pardonable hyperbole.

Carey, John. *A New Introduction to Lebor Gabála Érenn: The Book of the Taking of Ireland, Edited and Translated by R.A. Stewart Macalister.* Dublin: Irish Texts Society, 1993. A study by the world's leading expert on this vital text about the origins of the Irish.

Carson, Ciarán, trans. *The Táin: A New Translation of the Táin Bó Cúailnge.* London: Penguin Books, 2007. A wonderfully readable translation of the great Irish epic.

Carver, Martin. *Portmahomack: Monastery of the Picts.* Edinburgh: Edinburgh University Press, 2008. An account of the excavation of an important Pictish monastery in northern Scotland.

Celtic Congress. http://www.celtic-congress.org/.

Celtic League. https://www.celticleague.net/.

Collis, John. *The Celts: Origins, Myths, Inventions*. Stroud: Tempus, 2003. An account of how the concept of the Celt arose in European scholarship and popular culture, and of how it has come under increasing pressure from scholarly reassessment.

Conradh na Gaeilge (Gaelic League). https://www.cnag.ie/en/.

Cowan, Edward J., ed. *The Wallace Book*. Edinburgh: John Donald, 2007. A collection of articles that assess the career and impact of Sir William Wallace (protagonist of the film *Braveheart*).

Cross, Tom Peete, and Clark Harris Slover, eds. *Ancient Irish Tales*. Totowa, N. J.: Barnes and Noble Books, 1981. A collection of translations of key texts from the various Irish literary cycles.

Cunliffe, Barry. *Facing the Ocean: The Atlantic and Its Peoples, 8000 BC– AD 1500*. Oxford: Oxford University Press, 2001. A sweeping study of the Atlantic coast of Europe that supports the Celtic from the west model of the development of Celtic languages.

Cunliffe, Barry, and John T. Koch, eds. *Celtic from the West: Alternative Perspectives from Archaeology, Genetics, Language and Literature*. Oxford: Oxbow Books, 2010. The first of two volumes seeking to revolutionize the story of the origins of Celtic language and culture.

Davies, John. *A History of Wales*. London: The Penguin Press, 1990. A magisterial survey of Welsh history and culture from prehistory to modern times.

Dillon, Myles, and Nora K. Chadwick. *The Celtic Realms*. Second edition. London: Weidenfeld and Nicholson, 1972. A classic and still valuable survey of Celtic Britain and Ireland.

Duffy, Seán, ed. *Atlas of Irish History*. Second edition. Dublin: Gill and Macmillan, 1997. An invaluable series of historical maps with useful commentary.

———. *Robert the Bruce's Irish Wars: The Invasions of Ireland, 1306–1329*. Stroud: Tempus, 2002. A collection of articles about the Scottish invasion of Ireland in 1315–1318.

Duncan, Archibald A. M. *Scotland: The Making of the Kingdom*. New York: Barnes and Noble Books, 1975. A very thorough study of Scottish history from prehistory to 1300.

Ellis, Peter Berresford. *The Celtic Empire: The First Millennium of Celtic History, 1000 BC–51 AD*. Durham: Carolina Academic Press, 1990. A lucid narrative of the Celtic encounter with the classical world.

———. *The Cornish Language and Its Literature*. London: Routledge and Kegan Paul, 1974. A survey of Cornish literature and culture.

———. *Women in Celtic Society and Literature*. Grand Rapids: William B. Eerdmans Publishing Company, 1995. An avowedly optimistic view of the experience of women in Celtic societies.

Ellis, Steven. *Tudor Ireland: Crown, Community and the Conflict of Cultures, 1470–1603*. London and New York: Longman Group Limited, 1985. A useful survey of this period when the English government was attempting to solve the Irish question by a series of measures that ended in conquest.

Farley, Julia, and Fraser Hunter, eds. *Celts: Art and Identity*. London: The British Museum Press, 2015. The catalogue of a blockbuster exhibition in Edinburgh and London, with contributions by leading experts in various fields of Celtic studies.

Flanagan, Marie Therese. *Irish Society, Anglo-Norman Settlers, Angevin Kingship*. Oxford: Oxford University Press, 1989. An excellent study of the period before and during the English invasion of Ireland in the 12th century.

Fleming, Robin. *Britain after Rome: The Fall and Rise, 400 to 1070*. London: Penguin Books, 2010. A pathbreaking study that uses archaeology to discredit the idea of an Anglo-Saxon invasion of Britain and argues instead for relatively peaceful infiltration and assimilation.

Ford, Patrick K., ed. and trans. *The Mabinogi and Other Medieval Welsh Tales*. Berkeley and Los Angeles: University of California Press, 1977. An excellent translation of the Four Branches of the *Mabinogi*, plus several other Welsh tales.

Forsyth, David, ed. *Bonnie Prince Charlie and the Jacobites*. Edinburgh: NMS Enterprises, 2017. The catalogue of an exhibition on the Jacobites held at the National Museum of Scotland in Edinburgh, with excellent treatment of the Gaelic component of the Jacobite wars.

Frame, Robin. *Colonial Ireland, 1169–1369*. Second edition. Dublin: Four Courts Press, 2012. A concise and extremely helpful survey of Irish history in the two centuries after the initial English invasion.

———. *English Lordship in Ireland, 1318–1361*. Oxford: Clarendon Press, 1982. A detailed study of the English settler community during a period of tension and decline.

Freeman, Philip. *Ireland and the Classical World*. Austin: University of Texas Press, 2001. An invaluable study of every classical reference to Ireland.

———. *The Philosopher and the Druids: A Journey among the Ancient Celts*. New York: Simon and Schuster, 2006. A brilliant reconstruction of the voyages of Poseidonius, interwoven with penetrating insights about the classical sources for the Celts.

———. *War, Women, and Druids: Eyewitness Reports and Early Accounts of the Ancient Celts*. Austin: University of Texas Press, 2002. A compendium of classical texts about the Celts with incisive commentary.

Gaelic Athletic Association. http://www.gaa.ie/.

Galliou, Patrick, and Michael Jones. *The Bretons*. Oxford: Basil Blackwell, 1981. A comprehensive study of Breton history and culture from prehistory to modern times.

Gantz, Jeffrey, trans. *Early Irish Myths and Sagas*. Harmondsworth: Penguin Books, 1981.

Geoffrey of Monmouth, *The History of the Kings of Britain*. Translated by Lewis Thorpe. London: Penguin Books, 1977. One of the chief sources for the craze for Arthurian literature in medieval Europe.

Gerald of Wales. *Expugnatio Hibernica: The Conquest of Ireland*. Edited and translated by A. B. Scott and F. X. Martin. Dublin: Royal Irish Academy, 1978. The most detailed narrative source for the English conquest of Ireland.

———. *The History and Topography of Ireland*. Revised edition. Translated by John J. O'Meara. London: Penguin Books, 1982. A compendium of lore about Ireland containing many stereotypes that would influence English views of the Irish down to modern times.

Ghosh, Pallab. "DNA Study Shows Celts Are Not a Unique Genetic Group." BBC News, March 18, 2015. http://www.bbc.com/news/science-environment-31905764.

Gillingham, John. *The Angevin Empire*. Second edition. London: Arnold, 2001. An excellent treatment of the relationship between England and its neighbors in the 12th century.

Goscinny, Réné, and Albert Uderzo. *Asterix the Gaul*. Translated by Anthea Bell and Derek Hockridge. Revised edition. London: Orion Books, 2004. The first in a series of animated books about a fictional Gaulish village that continues to resist Roman rule.

Green, Miranda J., ed. *The Celtic World*. London and New York: Routledge, 1995. An invaluable compendium of themed chapters by scholars in every discipline related to the Celts.

Hoagland, Kathleen, ed. *1000 Years of Irish Poetry: The Gaelic and Anglo-Irish Poets from Pagan Times to the Present*. Old Greenwich, Conn.: The Devin-Adair Company, 1947. A comprehensive collection of Irish poetry written originally in Latin, Old Irish, and English.

"The Hochford/Enz Celtic Museum: A Find of the Century and Its Museum." Keltenmuseum Hochdorf/Enz. http://www.keltenmuseum.de/English/.

Hudson, Benjamin. *The Picts*. Oxford: Wiley Blackwell, 2014. An up-to-date survey of Pictish history and culture.

Jackson, Kenneth Hurlstone. *The Gododdin: The Oldest Scottish Poem*. Edinburgh: Edinburgh University Press, 1969. A translation with commentary of the first poem to mention Arthur by name.

———. *The Oldest Irish Tradition: A Window on the Iron Age*. Cambridge: Cambridge University Press, 1964. The classic formulation of the so-called nativist view of early Irish tradition.

James, Simon. *The Atlantic Celts: Ancient People or Modern Invention?* Madison: University of Wisconsin Press, 1999. An avowedly Celto-skeptical but sensible study of the Atlantic Iron Age, especially Britain.

———. *The World of the Celts*. New York: Thames and Hudson, 1993. A more traditional, lavishly illustrated treatment of the broader Celtic phenomenon.

Kelly, Fergus. *A Guide to Early Irish Law*. Dublin: Institute for Advanced Studies, 1988. An indispensable study of early Irish legal texts.

Koch, John T., ed., in collaboration with John Carey. *The Celtic Heroic Age: Literary Sources for Ancient Celtic Europe and Early Ireland and Wales*. Fourth edition. Aberystwyth: Celtic Studies Publications, 2003. A source reader covering both the continental Celts and Britain and Ireland.

Koch, John T., and Barry Cunliffe, eds. *Celtic from the West 2: Rethinking the Bronze Age and the Arrival of Indo-European in Atlantic Europe.* Oxford and Oakville: Oxbow Books, 2013. The second of two volumes that seek to revise the scholarly view of how Celtic language and culture developed.

Laing, Lloyd, and Jennifer Laing. *Celtic Britain and Ireland, AD 200–800: The Myth of the Dark Ages.* Dublin: Irish Academic Press, 1990. A heavily archeological study of Celtic Britain and Ireland.

Litton, Helen. *The Celts: An Illustrated History.* Dublin: Wolfhound Press, 1997. An excellent short guide to the Celts with copious photographs and drawings.

Livy. *The Early History of Rome.* Translated by Aubrey de Selincourt. London: Penguin Books, 2002. Contains the (somewhat contested) account of the Celtic sack of Rome in 390 B.C.

Loomis, Richard Morgan Loomis, ed. and trans. *Dafydd ap Gwilym: The Poems.* Binghampon, NY: Center for Medieval and Early Renaissance Studies, 1982. Still the best collection of Dafydd's poems in English.

Lucas, A. T. "Irish-Norse Relations: Time for a Reappraisal?," *Journal for the Cork Historical and Archaeological Society* 71 (1966): 62–75. A revisionist view of the impact of the Vikings in Ireland.

———. "The Plundering and Burning of Churches in Ireland, 7th to 16th Century." In *North Munster Studies: Essays in Commemoration of Monsignor Michael Moloney*, edited by Etienne Rynne, pp. 172–229. Limerick: Thomond Archaeological Society, 1967. A study that demonstrates that church burning was a routine activity in Ireland, by no means restricted to the Vikings.

Macaulay, Donald, ed. *The Celtic Languages.* Cambridge: Cambridge University Press, 1992. A study of the six surviving Celtic languages by experts in each language, with a brief but useful overview of the language family as a whole.

MacManus, Seumas. *The Story of the Irish Race*. Revised edition. Old Greenwich, CT: Devin-Adair, 1921. A classic Gaelic revival–era text, heavily influenced by *The Book of Invasions*.

Macpherson, James. *Ossian's Fingal*. New York: Woodstock Books, 1996. The text that sparked the greatest literary controversy of the 18th century: Were Ossian's poems genuine or forged?

Maund, Kari. *The Welsh Kings: Warriors, Warlords, and Princes*. Stroud: Tempus, 2006. A concise and helpful narrative of medieval Welsh history.

McCone, Kim. *Pagan Past and Christian Present in Early Irish Literature*. Naas, Co. Kildare: An Sagart, 1990. A study of the impact of Christianity on early Irish literature.

Megaw, Ruth, and Vincent Megaw. *Celtic Art: From Its Beginnings to the Book of Kells*. New York: Thames and Hudson, 1989. A beautifully illustrated volume that represents an older model of Celtic origins but contains still-valuable aesthetic interpretations of Celtic art.

Moody, T. W., F. X. Martin and F. J. Byrne, eds. *A New History of Ireland, Vol. III: Early Modern Ireland, 1534–1691*. Oxford: Oxford University Press, 1987. A very useful, detailed survey of the 16th and 17th centuries in Ireland.

Moody, T. W., F. X. Martin, and Dermot Keogh, eds., with Patrick Kiely. *The Course of Irish History*. Fifth edition. Lanham, MD: Roberts Rinehart, 2011. A helpful one-volume history of Ireland with chapters by experts in each period.

Nordenfalk, Carl. *Celtic and Anglo-Saxon Painting: Book Illumination in the British Isles, 600–800*. New York: George Braziller, 1977. A useful, brief survey of the high period of insular manuscript decoration.

Ó Báoill, Dónall. "Bardic Poetry." Wars and Conflict: The Plantation of Ulster. http://www.bbc.co.uk/history/british/plantation/bardic/index.shtml.

O'Connor, Ulick. *All the Olympians: A Biographical Portrait of the Irish Literary Renaissance.* New York: Atheneum, 1984. An elegant, very readable study of the major figures of the Gaelic revival.

Ó Corráin, Donncha. *Ireland before the Normans.* Dublin: Gill and Macmillan, 1972. An older but still valuable survey of Irish history and society before the English invasion of the 12th century.

Ó hAllmhuráin, Gearóid. *A Short History of Irish Traditional Music.* Dublin: The O'Brien Press, 2017. The single best short study of Irish music.

O'Meara, John J., trans. *The Voyage of Saint Brendan: Journey to the Promised Land.* Portlaoise: Dolmen Press, 1976. A translation of one of the seminal texts of the early Irish church.

Piggott, Stuart. *The Druids.* New York: Thames and Hudson, 1968. An older but still valuable survey of the druids.

Rankin, H. D. *Celts and the Classical World.* London and Sydney: Areopagitica Press, 1987. A study of the cultural exchanges between the Celts and their classical neighbors.

Rees, Alwyn, and Brinley Rees. *Celtic Heritage: Ancient Tradition in Ireland and Wales.* New York: Grove Press, 1961. A study of Celtic literature and mythology heavily influenced by the theory that Indo-European cultural patterns persisted into historic times.

Reilly, Gavan. "'A Úachtaráin, agus a Chairde'—Queen Offers 'Sincere Sympathy' to Victims of Anglo-Irish Conflict." TheJournal.ie. http://www.thejournal.ie/%E2%80%9Ca-uachtarain-agus-a-chairde%E2%80%9D-%E2%80%93-queen-offers-%E2%80%9Csincere-sympathy%E2%80%9D-to-victims-of-anglo-irish-conflict-139244-May2011/.

Renfrew, Colin. "Ethnogenesis: Who Were the Celts?" In *Archaeology and Language: The Puzzle of Indo-European Origins*, pp. 211–249. Cambridge: Cambridge University Press, 1987. An attempt to harmonize linguistic and archaeological evidence about the Celts.

Ritchie, Fiona, and Doug Orr. *Wayfaring Strangers: The Musical Journey from Scotland and Ulster to Appalachia*. Durham: The University of North Carolina Press, 2014. A fascinating study of the musical links between Scotland and Northern Ireland on the one hand, and Appalachia on the other, with an accompanying CD.

Russell, Paul. *An Introduction to the Celtic Languages*. London and New York: Longman, 1995. A detailed analysis of the features of the Celtic language family as a whole, as well as its main branches and individual languages.

Ryan, Philip. "Taoiseach Defends Appointment of Minister without Fluent Irish." Independent.ie. July 16, 2014. https://www.independent.ie/irish-news/politics/taoiseach-defends-appointment-of-gaeltacht-minister-without-fluent-irish-30436569.html.

The Secret of Kells. Directed by Tomm Moore and Nora Twomey. GKIDS, 2009. A beautiful animated film about creation and preservation of the *Book of Kells* that was nominated for numerous awards.

Sigerson, George, trans. *Bards of the Gael and Gall: Examples of the Poetic Literature of Erinn*, third edition. Dublin: Talbot Press, 1925. An old but still valuable collection of Irish poetry from the early Middle Ages to the modern period.

Simms, Katharine. *From Kings to Warlords: The Changing Political Structure of Gaelic Ireland in the Later Middle Ages*. Woodbridge: The Boydell Press, 1987. The best study of native Irish society in the late Middle Ages.

Skinner, John, trans. *The Confession of Saint Patrick and Letter to Coroticus*. New York: Image Books, 1998. A beautifully translated version of St. Patrick's two surviving works.

Spenser, Sir Edmund. *A View of the State of Ireland.* Edited by Andrew Hadfield and Willy Maley. Oxford: Blackwell Publishers, 1997. Spenser's infamous manifesto advocating the total conquest of Ireland.

Synge, John Millington. *The Complete Plays*. London: Methuen Drama, 2001. Contains some of the most influential plays of the Gaelic revival, including *Playboy of the Western World*.

Thomas, Charles. *Celtic Britain*. New York: Thames and Hudson, 1986. A well-illustrated survey of Britain from the end of Roman occupation to the advent of the Vikings.

Trevor-Roper, Hugh. "The Invention of Tradition: The Highland Tradition of Scotland." In *The Invention of Tradition*, edited by Eric Hobsbawm and Terence Ranger, pp. 15–41. Cambridge: Cambridge University Press, 1983. A seminal article arguing that many aspects of supposed Scottish tradition were "invented" in the late 18th and early 19th centuries, especially the concept of the clan tartan.

Whoriskey, Peter. "A Man's Discovery of Bones under His Pub Could Forever Change What We Know about the Irish." *Washington Post*, March 17, 2016. https://www.washingtonpost.com/news/wonk/wp/2016/03/17/a-mans-discovery-of-bones-under-his-pub-could-forever-change-what-we-know-about-the-irish/?utm_term=.382eedb184e7.

Wormald, Jenny, ed. *Scotland: A History*. Oxford: Oxford University Press, 2005. An excellent survey of Scottish history in a series of chapters by experts on each time period.

Yeats, William Butler. *Eleven Plays of William Butler Yeats*. Edited by A. Norman Jeffares. New York: Collier Books, 1964. Contains some of the most influential plays of the Gaelic Revival, including *Cathleen Ni Houlihan*.

❈ Image Credits ❈

Page No.

i	© CaoChunhai/iStock/Thinkstock.
vi	© javarman3/iStock/Thinkstock.
4	© revel.stockart/iStock/Thinkstock.
5	© ouchi_iro/iStock/Thinkstock.
5	© Joss/iStock/Thinkstock.
5	© Michael Burrell/iStock/Thinkstock.
6	© vivalapenler/iStock/Thinkstock.
17	© sedmak/iStock/Thinkstock.
18	© PanosKarapanagiotis/iStock/Thinkstock.
21	© sorsillo/iStock/Thinkstock.
26	Bender235/Wikimedia Commons/Public Domain.
28	Rosemania/Wikimedia Commons/CC BY 2.0.
29	Claude Valette/Wikimedia Commons/CC BY-SA 3.0.
31	KnudW/Wikimedia Commons/CC BY-SA 3.0.
44	Jll294~commonswiki/Wikimedia Commons/CC BY 3.0.
46	Library of Congress Prints and Photographs Division, LC-DIG-pga-03095.
47	© AndreaAstes/iStock/Thinkstock.
48	© Crisfotolux/iStock/Thinkstock.
56	AchilleT/Wikimedia Commons/Public Domain.
57	Jll294~commonswiki/Wikimedia Commons/CC BY-SA 3.0.
58	PicturePrince/Wikimedia Commons/CC BY-SA 4.0.
62	© Dorling Kindersley/Thinkstock.
66	Jorgeroyan/Wikimedia Commons/CC BY-SA 3.0.
69	DIREKTOR/Wikimedia Commons/CC BY 2.5.
71	© mjunsworth/iStock/Thinkstock.
73	AgTigress/Wikimedia Commons/CC BY-SA 3.0.
77	© MikkoMiettinen/iStock/Thinkstock.
78	Nheyob/Wikimedia Commons/CC BY-SA 4.0.
82	Catfish Jim and the soapdish/Wikimedia Commons/CC BY-SA 3.0.
88	Fæ/flickr/Wikimedia Commons.

90	© Wild_Strawberries/iStock/Thinkstock.
98	Library of Congress Prints and Photographs Division, LC-DIG-det-4a26185.
98	© Photos.com/Thinkstock.
104	© Celiaaa/iStock/Thinkstock.
105	Myrabella/Wikimedia Commons/CC BY-SA 4.0.
108	© GeorgiosArt/iStock/Thinkstock.
111	Jule_Berlin/flickr/CC BY-SA 2.0.
116	Sigehelmus/Wikimedia Commons/CC BY-SA 2.0.
117	Xenophon/Wikimedia Commons/CC BY-SA 3.0.
119	© Dorling Kindersley/Thinkstock.
125	© Photos.com/Thinkstock.
128	Kglavin/Wikimedia Commons/CC BY-SA 3.0.
129	© Photos.com/Thinkstock.
132	© mlschach/iStock/Thinkstock.
138	Fæ/flickr/Wikimedia Commons.
146	Teufelbeutel/Wikimedia Commons/CC BY-SA 4.0.
153	Blue Elf/Wikimedia Commons/CC BY-SA 2.0.
157	Marshallhenrie/Wikimedia Commons/CC BY-SA 3.0.
163	© dan_wrench/iStock/Thinkstock.
166	© Mustang_79/iStock/Thinkstock.
175	© Photos.com/Thinkstock.
176	© GeorgiosArt/Thinkstock.
179	Kjetilbjornsrud/Wikimedia Commons/CC BY 2.5.
181	© AarStudio/iStock/Thinkstock.
187	Rhion/Wikimedia Commons/Public Domain.
191	Seth Whales/Wikimedia Commons/Public Domain.
194	© Photos.com/Thinkstock.
200	© Photos.com/Thinkstock.
206	© Photos.com/Thinkstock.
208	© Ray Grinaway/Thinkstock.
216	Library of Congress Prints and Photographs Division, LC-DIG-pga-01749.
220	Library of Congress Prints and Photographs Division, LC-DIG-ggbain-06199.
221	Johnbod/Wikimedia Commons/CC BY-SA 3.0.
224	Xenophon/Wikimedia Commons/CC BY-SA 3.0.
225	David.Monniaux/Wikimedia Commons/CC BY-SA 3.0.
228	© MargoJH/iStock/Thinkstock.

237 .... Library of Congress Prints and Photographs Division, LC-USZ62-96046.
238 ....© Katiko/iStock/Thinkstock.
241..© Rawpixel/iStock/Thinkstock.

Notes

Notes

Notes

Notes

Notes

Notes

Notes